I0129599

The International Library of Sociology

HOW PEOPLE VOTE

Founded by KARL MANNHEIM

The International Library of Sociology

POLITICAL SOCIOLOGY
In 18 Volumes

HOW PEOPLE VOTE

A Study of Electoral Behaviour in Greenwich

by

MARK BENNEY,
A. P. GRAY and R. H. PEAR

Routledge
Taylor & Francis Group

LONDON AND NEW YORK

First published in 1956
by Routledge

Reprinted in 1998, 1999, 2000, 2001
by Routledge
2 Park Square, Milton Park, Abingdon, Oxon, OX14 4RN
711 Third Avenue, New York, NY 10017

Transferred to Digital Printing 2007

Routledge is an imprint of the Taylor & Francis Group, an informa business

First issued in paperback 2013

© 1956 Mark Benney, A. P. Gray and R. H. Pear

All rights reserved. No part of this book may be reprinted or reproduced
or utilized in any form or by any electronic, mechanical, or other means,
now known or hereafter invented, including photocopying
and recording, or in any information storage or retrieval system, without
permission in writing from the publishers.

The publishers have made every effort to contact authors/copyright holders
of the works reprinted in *The International Library of Sociology*.
This has not been possible in every case, however, and we would
welcome correspondence from those individuals/companies
we have been unable to trace.

British Library Cataloguing in Publication Data
A CIP catalogue record for this book
is available from the British Library

How People Vote
ISBN13: 978-0-415-17547-0 (hardback)
ISBN13: 978-0-415-86324-7 (paperback)

Political Sociology: 18 Volumes
ISBN 0-415-17820-7
The International Library of Sociology: 274 Volumes
ISBN 0-415-17838-X

Publisher's Note
The publisher has gone to great lengths to ensure the quality of this
reprint but points out that some imperfections in the original
may be apparent

CONTENTS

LIST OF TABLES

List of Tables

List of Tables

FOREWORD

THE investigation on which the following report has been based was initiated by a grant to the London School of Economics and Political Science by the Elmgrant Trust in 1948, for the purpose of conducting an inquiry into political behaviour. The Governors of the School appointed a committee, of which the late Professor Harold Laski was the original chairman, to supervise the investigation.

On Professor Laski's death I became chairman of the committee, the other members being Professor David Glass, Professor of Sociology in the University of London, Professor M. G. Kendall, Professor of Statistics in the University of London, Mr. Michael Young, Dr. Henry Durant of the British Institute of Public Opinion, Mr. T. Lewis and Mr. Mark Benney.

Mr. Benney was appointed to be Director of the Survey in July 1949. Mr. S. Oreanu acted as his assistant and was later succeeded by Mrs. P. Geiss. Mr. Benney's task was to formulate the criteria for the selection of the area in which the investigation was to be conducted. After careful consideration the committee adopted his recommendation that Greenwich should be the constituency in which political behaviour should be studied intensively.

The investigation was focused on the General Election which took place in February 1950. The method of inquiry involved sample interviews being made in three successive waves. This part of the work was entrusted to the British Institute of Public Opinion.

The sum of money originally made available by the Elmgrant Trust did not prove sufficient to cover the whole cost of the investigation and further sums were granted by the

xi

Department of Sociology and Demographic Research of the London School of Economics and Political Science and by the Governors of the London School of Economics, who also provided accommodation and other facilities for the staff. The British Institute of Public Opinion generously waived their claim to part of the remuneration which was due to them in respect of the work which they had carried out.

In August 1951, Mr. Benney went to the United States to take up a teaching post. Before leaving he had finished the drafts of Chapters One to Five inclusive; but was unable to complete the report. After some delay, the committee decided to appoint other workers in this field to do so. Mr. R. H. Pear and Miss A. P. Gray were willing to step into the breach, and the committee gratefully accepted their help. Miss Gray had excellent qualifications for continuing the work, as she had participated in the Elmira Investigation in America and had done post-graduate work in the Department of Sociology at Columbia University. Mr. Pear, who is a lecturer in Political Science at the London School of Economics, took on general responsibility for seeing that the work was brought to a conclusion, and has himself contributed the introduction. Miss Gray has contributed Chapters Six to Thirteen, together with the appendices A, B, C and D. She has also made a few necessary revisions in the earlier chapters. Mr. Benney subsequently read the entire report and made a number of corrections and comments. The work is thus a composite effort, but the actual writing is mainly attributable to Mr. Benney and Miss Gray.

All the members of the committee have read the typescript of the report.

A great deal of assistance was voluntarily given by nearly a hundred students who reported on various aspects of the political activities which took place in Greenwich during the election campaign. Thanks are due to them for their valuable help.

WILLIAM A. ROBSON.

London School of Economics
and Political Science.

INTRODUCTION

I N this survey we have tried to do two things. Firstly,
to describe in factual terms the constituency of Greenwich and the organisation of political parties there, and
to provide background material from the history of local and
national politics in the constituency, against which to describe the political events of the General Election of 1950.
Our second object has been to record the political interest,
activity, and preferences of Greenwich citizens, and to relate
these to characteristics of age, sex, social and economic
status, religion and education which it is reasonable to
regard as commonly associated with certain political attitudes. (The word 'associated' is used advisedly, for social
scientists have an understandable reluctance to enter into
an often unprofitable logical debate as to whether, and under
what conditions, observed facts which follow regularly or are
invariably associated with other observed facts, are really
caused by them.) To establish and analyse such facts and
associations, the questionnaire, the statistician (and nowa-
days the Hollerith machine) are essential aids to inquiry.
In theory there is no personal or social characteristic
which could not be recorded and related statistically to
political interest and activity, but we have chosen some of
those which seem *prima facie* to be relevant to a description
of the influences affecting voting habits and political activity.
We did not invent these characteristics of religion, economic
status, trade union membership and so on as devices for
analysing the make-up of political opinion. Before the days
of public opinion polling and social surveys there were adequate grounds for believing that these things were important.
We have done no more than apply recognised categories of

I   I

social characteristics to our panel of informants, and it is possible that other factors of which we are not aware ought to be brought into consideration in any future studies of this kind.[1]

As this was the first inquiry of its kind to be conducted in Great Britain,[2] something should be said of previous studies here and elsewhere. Studies of election figures, arithmetical calculations about the 'swing' of votes from one election to another, detailed accounts, from election figures, of how particular cities, counties or states changed their allegiance— all these are comparatively old and familiar. In countries where election ballots are not only cast but counted in the separate polling stations, it has been possible to attribute political preferences to certain social groups if the social make-up of the political sub-division was reasonably homogenous. For example in some American city precincts where votes are very few in number an active and intelligent precinct captain knows most of the voters personally and could estimate with reasonable accuracy how certain social groups would vote. Moreover, where official election returns are published for such smaller sub-divisions of a constituency, estimates of the relationships between social characteristics and vote preference can be offered by comparing the general characteristics of a residential area with the way it votes.[3] In this country where all votes are counted at the Town Hall or some other central point and general totals only are published, rather less can be done on these lines.[4] Any good agent or party worker could tell you which wards will vote Labour and which Conservative (and will have some hard facts from

[1] In the whole of this survey we have leant heavily on the techniques described in Paul Lazarsfeld's *The People's Choice* (2nd edition, 1948)—an inquiry into political behaviour conducted in Erie County, Ohio, during the Presidential Election of 1940. We also had the benefit of consultation with the directors of the Elmira (N.Y.) political survey of 1948, reported in B. R. Berelson's *Voting* (Chicago, 1954). In particular we borrowed heavily from the questionnaires of this survey.

[2] A similar inquiry was undertaken in Bristol, by political scientists from Bristol University, for the General Election of 1951. See R. S. Milne and H. C. Mackenzie, *Straight Fight* (Hansard Soc. 1954).

[3] See H. Tingsten, *Political Behaviour*.

[4] Voting totals for each polling station are available after the election, but not figures of party votes at each station.

local government elections to substantiate his views), but in a General Election the best estimate of this sort is a guess—often a very good guess. Canvassing before the election probably helps the guessing process, but our findings (and those of others) suggest that canvassing does not produce anything like an accurate forecast of how many votes will be cast for the party in the constituency.

We have been greatly assisted in our work by the invaluable Nuffield College studies of the general elections of 1945, 1950 and 1951,[1] and the reports of political scientists from Manchester University.[2] Mr. Nicholas's book in particular has been an essential work of reference for the picture of the national campaign of 1950. Our aim has been somewhat different, however. We took the fact of a national campaign for granted and concentrated upon the Greenwich voters in an attempt to discover who was affected by the national (and the local) campaign and how they were affected. 'Who' meant describing people in a variety of ways—men and women, young and old, rich and poor, well and ill educated, those 'interested in politics' and those not interested—and various combinations of these characteristics. 'How' means, for instance, whether or not they went to political meetings, read more newspapers, discussed politics more than usual, agreed or disagreed with party manifestos, wavered in their normal political allegiance, were reinforced in their political convictions, or decided to vote differently from 1945.

To carry out such an inquiry into personal conviction, activity and interest a 'panel' of interviewees can be chosen. The panel (which must be representative of the general mass of Greenwich voters) are then interviewed before, during and after the campaign, and on each occasion give answers to a lengthy questionnaire designed to extract from them information which the social scientists and statisticians

---

1 *The British General Election, 1945,* by R. B. McCallum and Alison Readman; *The British General Election of 1950* by H. G. Nicholas; *The British General Election of 1951* by D. E. Butler.
2 'Voting Behaviour in a Lancashire Constituency' by A. H. Birch and Peter Campbell, *British Journal of Sociology,* Vol. 1, p. 197; and 'Voting Behaviour in Droylesden in October 1951' by Peter Campbell, David Donnison and Allen Potter, *The Manchester School,* January 1952, p. 57.

regard as relevant for estimating their social characteristics, their political views and the effects on them of a period of sustained electioneering by the parties. The 'panel' technique is probably essential[1] in any inquiry which aims at finding out why people change (or do not change) their political views during a particular period of time. It gives a more than casual contact with a body of informants deemed to be representative of the whole body of constituents. But it is not a perfect method—some of the informants may be unavailable for interview when you want them (this will reduce the representativeness of the panel)—and it is a relatively expensive method of inquiry because it involves repeated interviews. As with other surveys it involves the careful preparation and pre-testing of questionnaires, the employment of trained interviewers (in our inquiry interviews were conducted by personnel of the British Institute of Public Opinion), the preparation from completed questionnaires of punch cards for the Hollerith machine, the advice of statisticians specialised in sampling techniques, and the employment of a trained operator for the machining of the cards. The amount of information which can be made available in this manner is only limited by common sense and considerations of cash. We hope that we were averagely endowed with the former and in this survey we cannot seriously claim that we did not have enough of the latter for the purpose we had in mind.

The first use of the face-to-face interview with a large number of voters[2] as a device for discovering facts of political interest and preference was probably that of Professors Merriam and Gosnell in Chicago in 1924 when they decided to find out the causes of non-voting in that city. Since then political opinion polling has (in spite of an unfortunate forecast of the American Presidential election in 1948) become an accepted part of the political scene that is scanned more or less anxiously by politicians and electors. The question which may be asked is: What is the use of all this informa-

---

[1] See Lazarsfeld, *The Use of Panels in Social Research* (Oslo, 1948); and in Marie Jahoda and others *Research Methods in Social Relations*, 1951.
[2] Actually non-voters. C. E. Merriam and H. F. Gossell, *Non-Voting*, 1924.

tion? The answers can only be tentative and partial. It may, and probably does, interest working politicians. Does that mean that if and when the statesman is adequately equipped with these modern devices he can so gauge the political temper of the nation (and adjust his party pronouncements accordingly) that he will always get the voting support he needs? It could, with certain politicians and in certain circumstances, mean just that, and many conscientious citizens find such a prospect horrifying. On the other hand some democratically minded people have urged the extended use of public opinion polls as being more reliable guides to what the public wants than General Elections—in other words, if democratic government aims at giving people what they want, their desires can be known most accurately by polling. The objections then come from those who do not agree that the purpose of government lies in giving the people what they want.

Nothing that we have done in this survey is designed to give particular encouragement to any of these points of view. Opinion polling has existed in this country for nearly twenty years, and its practical usefulness is now recognised by governments, of whatever colour, as an essential aid in planning and checking upon the efficiency of various services which the taxpayer supports for his own benefit. There is no difficulty in defending the use of surveys for such practical purposes. Of their usefulness to students of political science (and of political theory) much could be written, and there are those who suggest that the discovery of the psychological roots of political behaviour has (or should) completely upset the orthodox teaching of political theory. In 1908 Graham Wallas[1] described how political opinion was formed not always upon a basis of rational choice between clear alternatives, but more often through a non-rational identification of citizens with indefinable symbols of patriotism, party sentiment or other emotionally charged banners and devices. Wallas, who wanted rationality wherever possible, put great stress upon the power of education to steer ordinary men into the paths of rationality. There is (to anticipate our report)

[1] *Human Nature in Politics.*

5

little to show that some four decades after men are now more rational in this sense than before. In fact those whose *political* education is highest often show both the highest degree of loyalty to the party, *and* the greatest disagreement with the party's programme. (This will not surprise any reader who is an observer of, or a participant in, the work of a local Labour Party, or a Young Conservative organisation.) This suggests at once that the test or characteristic of rationality may be in need of revision, or perhaps should be altogether discarded, for in another sense (one which involves a good deal of reflection upon one's own and the party's experience and a similar amount of speculation about the political future) it may be quite rational to vote for the party because you discern within its thinking or past performance something which gives hope for the future, even although you disagree with most of its current manifesto. What does seem clear is that most of our informants voted for what they considered their class interests. They allocated themselves (not always accurately by 'objective' tests) to a certain social class and voted for what seemed best for their class. This does not mean that all Englishmen are at heart convinced Marxists, for we have no evidence to suggest that they envisage an eventual class war to settle class differences once and for all. It probably means no more than that they, in their way, agree with the views of sociologists (British and foreign) that of all the democracies, England is the one in which there is the most consciousness of class and most awareness of class distinctions and the pattern of social intercourse which flows therefrom. It may be urged therefore that, whether or not it be immoral or incorrect to vote one's class interest, it is not a sufficient or an obvious condemnation to say that voting on class lines is not rational. To one who believes that he will benefit if his class does (and that political effort should be applied to benefiting people like himself) it is wholly rational to vote on class lines.[1]

Sir Ernest Barker once criticised writers who stressed the irrational elements in politics by saying: 'This is to explain

[1] See, e.g., F. Zweig, *Labour, Life and Poverty.*

society as an irrational structure and therefore not to explain society at all.'[1]

Sociologists and some political scientists are continually drawing attention to the irrational sources of political and social behaviour and to the complexity and untidiness of the processes of government and politics.[2] We may or may not agree with Sir Ernest Barker, but it is undoubtedly true that the teaching process for academics is much smoother if we assume that society is a 'rational structure' and that political choice and political theory can be taught and learnt in terms of rational thinkers and rational citizens. We would not urge that the classic approach to political education be abolished, for whether or not (like micro-economics) it bears a close resemblance to the real world, it is a part of our culture, it stimulates thought on political topics and it is the sort of intellectual training which is probably of considerable use when one ventures into the field of political behaviour. Moreover political sociologists are in some sense testing orthodox themes as much as they are endeavouring to create new concepts. Political sociologists have not as yet produced a body of political theory which is as clear, attractive and communicable to the mass of intelligent people as the theories of the political scientists. They are producing data which illuminate and to a large extent criticise the older political theory. Their problem is, to quote Lazarsfeld,[3] the 'systematic integration of the data into a theoretical context', and they will probably solve it in time. (If it were not for the fact that their language because technical is still strange to many readers and that therefore they have not yet a large popular following, it could be said that they had already solved many of their problems.)

To return to the material of our survey. This consists of answers our informants gave to particular questions. We have to assume that these were truthful answers (and there are methods by which pollsters can detect any gross degree of lying on the part of informants—or interviewers). But even

1 Ernest Barker, *Political Thought in England, 1948–1814*, 2nd ed., p. 130.
2 See, e.g., David Truman, *The Governmental Process*.
3 Introduction to 2nd edition, *The People's Choice*, 1948.

so it is necessary to point out that we were asking important questions some of which are based on what the informants said they had done five years previously. Most people would in these circumstances answer truthfully—there is no particular reason why large numbers should lie, but it is always possible for people to forget how they voted in 1945. We cannot check for such aberrations. When you ask people how they will vote in the near future, again your answers may not be a wholly accurate forecast of actual voting. On the whole the nearer polling day you put this question the more likely it is to be reliable. Then we must bear in mind that what we discovered about political activity, interest and preference, was discovered during an election period when it is reasonable to assume that some voters feel, more than at other times, that they ought to have an interest in political questions. The pattern of political life and belief which we describe was that of a particular constituency during the last days of 1949 and up to Election Day in February 1950. Other constituencies at the same time, and this one at other times, could look different. A General Election period is a climax in the life of the party, locally and nationally, and no effort is spared by the parties to persuade the voters that it is the most important moment in their lives also. What, ideally, we should now do is to take our investigatory apparatus back to Greenwich in a non-election period and find out how our informants are responding to the more humdrum local political life when parties are ticking over in an ordinary fashion waiting for the next contest. Unless and until that is done our picture of political man and his interests cannot be regarded as a sufficiently substantial basis upon which to erect theoretical frameworks.

Finally there is the question of the election itself. It was an important election. It was the opportunity the voter had to support further 'welfare' policies of the Labour Government, but it was not at the same time an opportunity to pronounce in favour of dismantling the Welfare State, for the Conservatives were not committed to that policy. The historians of the future may well regard it as not a particularly memorable occasion, and the national verdict was not dramatic.

8

Introduction

There can be no such thing as a typical General Election, but we must bear in mind some of the characteristics of this particular political occasion[1] in reading the account which follows of the political aspects of life in Greenwich at the time of the General Election of 1950.

[1] See on this H. G. Nicholas's *The British General Election of 1950*.

Chapter One

BACKGROUND TO A SURVEY

THIS study presents the findings of a survey of political·
activities made in the borough of Greenwich before,
during and after the General Election of 1950.
The subject-matter is politics, but the aims are not political. Rather the basic concern of the work is sociological. We
are interested in the translation of private opinion into public
action and inaction; in the social processes by which power,
latent and dispersed throughout the electorate after a dissolution of Parliament, becomes again political power manifest and organised. But we are not concerned here with the
results of public action or the uses to which organised political
power is put.

Since this distinction between political and sociological
concerns may seem to impose arbitrary limits to the interests
of political science, it is worthwhile to pursue it further.
Students of politics use as their raw material all events arising
from efforts to influence and control the apparatus of State;
and a General Election is certainly an event of that order.
But every study imposes its own discipline. Political scientists,
concerned with the modes and distribution of power, have
rightly concentrated on those events where the forces involved are seen in their purest form. They have sought—
though not always consciously in Max Weber's sense—for
the 'ideal types' of manifest power. Wars and revolutions
have set the patterns of their thinking; statesmen and generals
have peopled their minds. Within this framework, even when
attention is distributed impartially between the contestants,

records of success survive in greater abundance than records of failure, and the resulting studies have a partial and uncertain character. To cite an obvious example, there are two dozen books available that describe the rise to power in this country of the Labour Party; there is not a single full-scale study of the decline of the Liberal Party.

In many accounts of British political institutions it will be asserted, of course, that power flows from the people. But how it flows, and why it flows in one direction and not another, are questions to which answers have been attempted only in the most general and tentative terms.[1] It is the Cabinets directing and applying the power that are minutely studied; and it has been the more easy to ignore sources of power since Ministers have been, almost by definition, the politicians who are given safe seats. The result has been that scarcely any of our institutions have received less detailed attention than our elections. The Reform Acts of the nineteenth century have been studied, but not the fateful elections that followed them. The strategies of dissolution, the bickerings and banterings of Cabinet-making, have been described from a hundred viewpoints; but of the intervals between dissolutions and the formation of Cabinets we know next to nothing.

'It is always to be lamented,' Burke told the House of Commons, 'when men are driven to search into the foundations of the Commonwealth.'[2] And if what we have been saying indicates a failure of political science, part of the blame, doubtless, must be attributed to this general reluctance to look gift horses in the mouth. But part of the blame rests also with the political scientist's audience, and the demands it makes on its scholars. Political history and commentary have been expected to establish for us the continuity of events, and to extract from them underlying patterns of dependency. We have required it to relate yesterday and to-day as cause and effect, to demonstrate for us how the

[1] This remark is intended to apply only to this country, of course. In France, in Sweden, in the United States the study of elections and electorates has a long history.

[2] 8 May, 1780. Speech given in C. S. Emden, *Selected Speeches on the Constitution*, Vol. II, p. 113.

contents of the morning paper should be viewed in the perspective of secular trends. Such an emphasis tempts the theorist to smooth the curves of change, to ignore the abrupt and discontinuous. From such a viewpoint a General Election becomes at best a punctuation point, an event to divide chapters. At worst it is an interruption, a change or break of trend, an event that requires the invocation of that shrouded and elusive deity, 'public opinion'. Thus whether the political philosopher has his eye on the forms of power or the continuity of events, in either case the electorate is likely to be overlooked.

There was a time—and it was then that the classic themes of democratic theory were established—when such oversights did little violence to the facts. Until well on towards the end of the nineteenth century the wielders of power were still relatively independent of direct electoral favour. Occasionally a statesman might have to scurry around the country in search of a safer seat—Gladstone was forced to on more than one occasion—but it was rare for even a commoner of prominence to have to contest his place in Parliament. Progressive extensions of the franchise reduced the number of unopposed returns from a half to a quarter of the total seats; but as late as 1900 we find, in a General Election with 670 places at stake, 240 of them uncontested, and an incoming Cabinet of eighteen members only three of whom had had to submit themselves to the ordeal of the ballot box. Such a Ministry might feel obliged to the electorate for office, but not for its whole political being. It was, in fact, likely to draw a sharp distinction between the electorate and 'public opinion'. The party machines could control the smaller electorates of those days. They could not control or ignore such organised pressure groups as the Anti-Corn Law League, the National Reform League, the Tariff Reform League or the Suffragette Movement—all bodies drawing on forces outside the electoral system. It was the inability of the Liberal Party to cope with the pressures exerted by the trade unions that led directly to the formation of the Labour Party.

Our very phrase—'public opinion'—carries with it semantic nuances from this era. The word *public*, with its strong overtones of contrast with *private*, suggests a group of people who are outsiders rather than insiders; and that in turn carries fainter meanings of a kind of spectator relationship to issues rather than an active one, a sense of distance from the source of power rather than nearness to it. In the word *opinion* we can find other underlying references at work. In some sense it contrasts with *knowledge*, echoing the old Platonic distinction between the eternal, immutable world of reality and the fluid, deceptive world of appearances. It becomes easy to put these multiple meanings together and arrive at a view of the parliamentary statesman, in Maine's phrase, 'listening nervously at one end of a speaking-tube which receives at its other end the suggestions of a lower intelligence'.[1] But we also use the phrase 'public opinion' with some vague sense of contrast to established authority or constitutional representation. There is still something of a radical atmosphere surrounding the phrase, a shadow of the disinherited and unrepresented, so that it implies attitudes to issues that haven't yet found their way into party programmes, attitudes of people who aren't on any voters' lists, and—most relevant in these days—the views of the '49%' who voted against the government in power. It was in this latter sense that Snowden used it when he acknowledged that 'no Government can move far ahead of public opinion'[2]; and this shift in the meaning of the phrase since Rousseau first introduced it helps us to assess some of the political change that has occurred within the lifetime of the average voter.

It is tempting to sum up this change by saying that there was a time when the expression of public opinion led to more democratic institutions, whereas to-day it leads to more public relations officers. If there is any modicum of truth in this statement, it is the consequence of the great broadening of the suffrage after the First World War. The five General Elections which have taken place since the establishment of universal suffrage have been radically different from all preceding ones, and the most fundamental difference is that 'public opinion' and the electorate have now become virtu-

[1] Sir Henry Maine, *Popular Government* (London, 1886), p. 38.
[2] Philip Snowden, *An Autobiography*, Vol. 1, p. 88.

ally synonymous. There can no longer be, as there was in the days of Cobden and Bright, a potentially effective body of public opinion outside the electoral system. It follows that, to the extent the parties can control electoral processes, they have effective control of public opinion as well; and the chances for any public to express its opinion on an issue that the parties choose not to regard as one diminish.

Other differences proceed from this. There is the new conception of party discipline which intrudes between a Member's conscience and the wishes of his constituents the menacing image of the party whip. There is a standardising of policies and personalities, so that during an election campaign indistinguishable candidates say indistinguishable kinds of things in every corner of the land. There is the changed attitude to the 'mandate'—a marked tendency to regard a programme accepted by the electorate as a set of rigid instructions to the successful Ministry. The extension of campaigning into even the most hopeless constituencies is changing the character of the campaign itself; for in these circumstances, as Tingsten has noted,[1] the parties not only direct their energies to arousing the interest of politically indifferent groups but they devote more and more effort to winning over voters from the opposing camp. Thus we tend to get a sharpened cleavage between the choices offered to the country, bringing into question not only who shall govern but how and what; and if the cleavage is sometimes implied rather than overtly stated, the tendency is still encouraged, in the electoral mind, to extend the concept of causation until all human good and evil becomes consequent upon political action.

It seems unlikely that the changes we have noted will exhaust the remoter consequences of universal suffrage. Bagehot, referring in 1872 to the effects of the Reform Act of 1867, remarked: 'A new constitution does not produce its full effect as long as all its subjects were reared under an old constitution, as long as its statesmen were trained by that old constitution. It is not really tested till it comes to be worked by statesmen and among a people neither of whom are guided

[1] H. Tingsten, *Political Behaviour* (Stockholm, 1937), p. 225.

15

by a different experience.'[1] As our elder statesmen retire, and our older voters pass with them, we can expect the pace of change to be accelerated rather than slowed down. Whether we can control the rate and direction of these changes will depend largely on our understanding of the social processes at work. Certainly it is not enough to explain them, as the tendency now is, in terms of the eclipse of the Liberal Party by the Labour Party. We need to pay more attention to the dull and simple arithmetic of majorities. The electorate is now virtually co-extensive with the adult population: a population that varies in regional interest and social composition, and is continually redistributing itself around the country. A periodic redistribution of electoral boundaries ensures that there will be a rough numerical equality between one constituency and another, but the boundary commissioners can take no stock of economic and social differences between one group of voters and another. As Mr. Butler has pointed out in his pioneering work on the electoral system,[2] the last redistribution of seats (1948), unimpeachably fair though it was, sent the Labour Party into the 1950 election with a handicap of something like half a million votes, or some thirty seats, precisely because of the *social* distribution of the Labour vote. With the development of adequate statistical techniques we can predict such biases, and if necessary control them; it seems unlikely such sociological factors will ever expose the powerful parties of to-day to such sudden and crushing defeats as that suffered by the Liberal Party in 1924. The danger to political stability, if there is one, comes rather from the nature of the electoral mind and the communication system that the parties are developing to influence it.

The tradition of political science can hardly be expected to provide insights into this problem, for it is one of social psychology and not of governmental forms. It concerns the attitudes and perceptions of individuals, the influences which affect their personal political decisions, their ideas of what a

[1] Walter Bagehot, *The British Constitution* (London, 1872, 2nd ed.), pp. ix.
[2] D. E. Butler, *The Electoral System in Britain: 1918–1951* (Oxford, 1953), pp. 195, 211.

16

vote entails, the private hopes and fears which they bring with them into the polling booths. It concerns the relation which this isolated political act bears to all the other activities in the individual life-cycle. At this level of investigation the questions asked will range beyond the strictly political, as this is customarily defined, and will not always seem relevant to the politician's problems as he has been accustomed to state them. The techniques of investigation and analysis used will be unfamiliar, and therefore perhaps repulsive, to political scientists. But unless the questions are asked and the techniques applied, the theory of politics will be in growing danger of attrition.

Implied here is a distinction between the public universe of politics and the millions of private universes of the electors. It is the basic purpose of this study to compare the kinds of universes and see in what respects they differ, and why.

To do this adequately involves, first, an attempt to define the public universe of politics. Since our frame of reference is a General Election the problem is less one of content than of perspective. There is not one public, but several, engaged publicly and professionally in politics, and each of them regards an election from a different level of abstraction. Journalists impose their image of the occasion on their public; political analysts build a background of assumptions and preconceptions for the journalists; constitutional historians create a framework of ideas within which the analyst works—and so on. These levels are not easily or precisely to be defined, either in terms of their relative abstractness or of their public, but they may be roughly classified into four groups.

The most abstract view of a General Election is that of the constitutional lawyer, who sees the occasion as one where a number of qualified electors choose a qualified representative to voice their concerns in the legislature.[1] The great web

---

[1] 'The principles of constitutional law recognised by the courts recognise the constitution of the Revolution settlement. Institutions and practices which have grown up since that time have not received formal recognition by the courts, and the rules relating to them are not part of the common law.' Ivor Jennings, *The Law and the Constitution* (London, 1948, 3rd ed.), p. 112. In view of the theories of representation current in 1688, there may be some doubt as to whether an elected Member is representing people or property.

of legal safeguards and sanctions which envelops a parliamentary election is a systematic projection of this viewpoint. It involves certain unexpressed assumptions about the nature of the electoral process. About the candidate it assumes that anyone with a serious belief in his fitness to represent the people (or their property), and who can persuade ten residents to sponsor him, can and will present himself for election in the constituency where his chances are greatest. About the electors it is assumed that each has an equal voice in the balloting, and that they are equally rational beings who need only to be shielded from bribery, impersonation and violence to arrive at a just choice.

A scarcely less abstract level of approach is that of the constitutional historian. From this viewpoint a General Election appears as a recurrent figure in the dance of four stately entities—the Crown, the Ministry, Parliament and the People. In this figure three of the entities are retiring to the point of passivity, and only the Ministry is the focus of attention. Parliament is dissolved when a Ministry fails to retain its confidence or when the people's mandate has grown weak with age. Following dissolution comes the General Election, a device for renewing the authority of the former Ministry or transferring it to a new one. Legitimate power emanates from the people, and this is the occasion when it is delegated, canalised and transformed into legitimate authority.

At these austere levels of vision, it is clear, the features commonly regarded as typical of a contemporary election are lost to view, and we have to lower our brows to the level of the political analyst before we can bring the political parties into the picture. It is the parties that bring to the occasion that element of conflict which is lost in the remoteness of constitutional perspectives. At this level, the General Election becomes a contest of organisations and issues—but with the organisations, in general, personified by their leaders. The parties formulate policies, and try to ensure that every elector is made favourably aware of them. The parties endorse candidates, lending them authority and strength in return for loyalty, and try to ensure that every

18

elector has a chance to vote for one of them. The parties choose leaders to form a possible Ministry, and by advertising their superior judgment, efficiency, moral strength and unity, strive to persuade every elector that they alone can be trusted with the reins of government. The parties are complex and continuing organisations, and their role at a General Election is only an intensification of their role at other times.

The wider the public for which a viewpoint has been formulated, the more complex and less internally consistent it becomes. The publicist's and journalist's view of an election is as much an aspect of the public universe of politics as those already dealt with; but it becomes coloured by the polemics it describes. Some common elements can be discerned, however, even among publicists of opposing parties. All see the occasion as an ideological one, an interpenetrating play between rival policies and public opinion. On the one hand, the public debate of the parties is seen as a way of educating the electorate to a fuller understanding of the national needs and interests. On the other hand, public opinion, after it has been enriched by this experience, is not only enabled to choose its government more wisely, it can also support it in office with understanding and tolerance. Informing this viewpoint are a number of scarcely concealed assumptions about political issues and public opinion. About the issues it is assumed that they will be confined to those presentable in terms which a non-expert person can comprehend and evaluate—all other issues are 'non-party' issues and will (or should) be left to experts. About public opinion it is assumed that there is already some consensus of agreement between the various group interests and attitudes included under that term, and that this agreement can be broadened and strengthened by rational discussion.

But there is another element of the publicist's view which requires attention, because it indicates a certain uneasiness about the assumption on which it is built. It is a view that comes into prominence only during a General Election. The occasion is seen as a crude and boisterous spectacle, not to be taken too seriously. Emphasis is laid on its saturnalian aspects —the slanging matches between statesmen and hecklers, the freak candidates, the 'incidents'. A reserve vocabulary is brought into play, of hustings and baby-kissing and soap-boxes and stunts and floating voters. From a hundred sources —cartoons, jokes, candid photographs, satirical articles— the image issues forth of an occasion when the citizen will do his duty lightheartedly and without expecting too much in the way of results. All this is obviously (if unconsciously) de-signed to reduce the level of tensions which an electoral con-flict might produce. It aims to create an atmosphere in which a healthy partisanship can flourish without endangering social ties. This too is a familiar aspect of the public universe of politics, and one of which we shall have to take account.

The point at which this many-imaged public likeness of a General Election meets and mingles with the private versions of the electors is the constituency. It is here that abstractions take on flesh and colour and context. It is here that the man-in-the-street lives. If ever politics becomes sensible and familiar to the ordinary man and woman, it is in the con-stituency, where leading articles are associated with the taste of marmalade, and Russia is something to talk about in the tea-break, and parties are people who ring your door-bell in the middle of your favourite radio programme, and an M.P. is someone who might help Dad to get his pension. But even a constituency is an abstraction to most people, who are aware only of living in a house in a street so many minutes from the shops and buses of the neighbourhood. And if a con-stituency is too big and artificial a unit for the ordinary elector to feel at home in, it is scarcely less so for the research-worker. In the designing of this survey it was necessary, if we were to have objective tests of our accuracy, to base our studies on a constituency, since that is the smallest unit for which official poll-returns are made. But we also wanted to carry out our research in the kind of locality where people are aware of their neighbours in a sense more extensive than is usual in the vicinity of London. In choosing a constituency, therefore, our first criterion was that its boundaries should have remained unchanged by the 1948 redistribution. This would enable us to compare past election returns with present, and extend the time-dimension of the survey. It would also reduce the possible confusions arising when people who voted in one constituency for a particular candidate in 1945 found themselves, as the victims of a redistribution, voting in another constituency with unfamiliar candidates in 1950.

A second criterion was that our constituency should have a diverse social composition. We were not looking for a 'typical' constituency—since property qualifications were abolished there has been no such thing. But we wanted to get as wide a variety of people as possible into our net. There were not resources enough to do as we might have wished—study a safe Tory seat such as Twickenham, and a safe Labour seat such as Poplar, and add a marginal constituency like West Woolwich. Instead we sought a constituency with the salient characteristics of each, where there were safe wards of different complexions, and marginal wards where the local parties fought it out.

A third important criterion was that the constituency should be contested by three parties, with the third preferably Liberal. We are so used to thinking in terms of the 'two-party' system that it is easy to forget how rarely we vote in those terms. Over the country as a whole, since the beginning of the century, there have more often been three or more names on a ballot-paper than two. And with the Liberal and Communist parties announcing grandiose election plans at the time we were planning the survey there was every reason to suppose this would be no less true in 1950. If the average voter were to be faced with a choice of three candidates, so too must be the voters we studied.

Fourth, we wanted a constituency the political history and social growth of which promised a relatively large 'floating vote'. In the London area, of course, such constituencies are becoming rarer. The usual measure of electoral swing is between one election and the next; and with a ten-year gap between the two previous elections, to say nothing of a world war, this measure was more than usually unreliable. Failing an extensive preliminary investigation of several constituencies, we had to settle for any division where the average turnover of votes was not lower than 18%—the figure for the whole Greater London area in 1945.

Our fifth criterion, too, was a pious hope rather than a firm touchstone. We wanted such political organisations as we studied to be typical of their kind. But since we had no way of knowing what are the characteristics of a 'typical' constituency party, we had to seek the advice of the Party headquarters.

Greenwich was the only constituency in the London area to meet the first four conditions we had laid down. As to the fifth condition, the two major parties were represented locally by active, vigorous bodies with large memberships (although one of them later developed schismatic troubles of a kind to hamper seriously its working efficiency). We had, in fact, little option but to conduct our inquiry in Greenwich.

The constitutional freedom which allows a Ministry to dissolve Parliament when it feels its mandate is exhausted, and which therefore introduces an element of grand strategy into the precise timing of an election, makes for certain difficulties in the planning of electoral research. We wanted to learn more about the formation of political attitudes and opinions than the normal polling technique of successive samplings of different people could tell us; it was our intention (following a well-known model[1]) to try to study fluctuations of opinion by repeated interviewing of the same sample of voters. We wanted to conduct three interviews with each informant— one in the relative quiet of normal pre-election conditions, one during the three weeks of election campaigning, and the last immediately after the election. But when should we begin our first wave of interviews? The latest possible date for the dissolution was the summer of 1950, but tactical reasons might induce the Prime Minister to make his appeal to the country on any day before that. We decided to gamble on the probability of a Spring election, and to conduct our first interviews towards the end of December 1949 in the reasonable hope that a period of three months or so would elapse before re-interviewing would be required. In the event, a

[1] Paul F. Lazarsfeld *et al.*, *The People's Choice* (N.Y. 1944).

bare seven weeks elapsed between the completion of the first wave of interviews and the initiation of the second.

A General Election offers a unique occasion for such studies of opinion and attitude formation, as valuable to the social psychologist as a solar eclipse is to the astronomer. It is one of the rare opportunities afforded to a social student to study a human community under conditions approximating to laboratory controls. Broadly speaking, the whole population is exposed to the same stimuli for the same period during the course of an election campaign, and the responses are expressed simultaneously in a narrowly limited range of simple acts designed to be counted. Knowing the distribution of political opinion before a campaign starts, and the distribution of votes after the balloting is done, you can examine in detail the relation of one to the other. If one has these data about a representative sample of people, and can interpose information about precisely who was exposed to the various campaign stimulants, then you can go further and examine the relations of public political activities to individual changes of opinion and behaviour.

These were the considerations that dictated the plan oɩ our survey so far as the electorate was concerned. From the Greenwich electoral register we selected every sixtieth name, and so obtained a sample of 1,022 persons that was in all practical respects random. These were interviewed for the first time at a period of comparative political quiescence— the two weeks preceding the Christmas holidays of 1949, and the two weeks following. Of course we were unsuccessful in reaching every person on our list. No electoral register is ever completely accurate, and among the names on our list were 65 who were dead, or had removed from the district, or whose names were there by error. This reduced the effective sample to 957 people, and of these we succeeded in interviewing 856. Most of the missing people were in hospitals or in occupations which took them away a good deal; some of them we managed to catch on the third interview. Only 26 people, less than 3% of the effective sample, positively refused to be interviewed.

The questionnaire used on this occasion was designed to

obtain, in addition to the usual demographic data, the past voting history of the individual, the extent of his political interest and information, and a variety of attitudinal material relating to policies, parties and sources of political intelligence.

Our research funds did not allow for a complete re-interviewing of the entire sample during the election campaign. Instead we selected, from among those interviewed in December, a number of sub-samples. We were interested in changes of opinion, and therefore included all those whose vote intention for the coming election differed ·from their 1945 vote. We also included all who had been too young to vote in 1945, and all Liberal supporters not otherwise included. To these were added all the 'undecided' people, and random selections of consistent Labour and Conservative supporters. The total selected for a second interview was 450 cases.

It was impracticable to conduct so many interviews all on the eve-of-poll, although, in an attempt to assess the effects of exposure to the campaign, this would have been desirable. In fact the interviewing was confined to the last ten days of the campaign, and even this relatively ample time limit led to heavy losses. In the two months that had elapsed since our last interview, 10 more people on our reduced lists had died or removed or gone abroad; and of the remaining 440 we were successful in catching 363 at their homes.

The questionnaire used for this second interview was designed to provide material about the individual's exposure to the various kinds of campaign activities, and the impact and effect. Where there had been changes in vote intention since the previous interview, these were systematically investigated.

The third interview, conducted within the week following polling day, again returned to the full sample. Once again by the time we got round, another 6 people had died, removed or gone abroad, and by making up to four calls on each address 839 people were interviewed. This time, although we failed to reach some people who had been interviewed earlier, we also reached others who had eluded us in December. All in all, of the 957 people whom we might have interviewed, we actually made contact with 914 on at least one occasion. The total losses from the effective sample were thus less than 5%. The following table summarises the results of the interviewing:

Table 1

SUMMARY OF INTERVIEWING RESULTS

Inquiry	No. drawn in sample	Deaths, Errors, Removals	Effective sample	Interviews obtained
Dec.–Jan.	1,022	65	957	856
Pre-poll	450	10	440	363
Post-poll	1,022	81	941	839

Persons receiving first interview only	49
,, ,, 1st and 2nd only	26
,, ,, 1st, 2nd and 3rd	337
,, ,, 1st and 3rd only	444
,, ,, 3rd only	58
Total of all persons interviewed	914

The sampling, interviewing and much of the detailed construction of questionnaires were carried out by the British Institute of Public Opinion, whose director, Mr. Henry Durant, and assistant director, Mr. Anthony Lewis, placed at our disposal a fund of research experience without which the project could scarcely have succeeded.

From these repeated interviews with a random sample of electors we obtained a picture—not perhaps as clear as we would have wished, but certainly voluminous in its detail—of the private processes of political thinking and choosing that went on behind the front doors of Greenwich. But how these were related to, how these influenced or were influenced by, the various public group activities that went on in committee rooms, meeting halls and party offices we were scarcely yet in a position to say. When we talk of an election 'campaign', what exactly do we mean? Who are the people who form themselves into political groups and try to persuade

25

others to their way of thinking? Why do they distribute their energies in one way rather than another? What are they trying to do, and why? What are the specific differences, if any, between a party's national campaign and its local inter-pretation by a candidate with his electors before his eyes?

Study of these questions required a separate inquiry, using quite other methods of research. Since interest was here focused on organisations rather than on individuals, our units of study were events rather than opinions, relations rather than intentions. These have to be described by the research-worker, and leave room for much subjective bias. Since we could not hope to eliminate bias we tried instead to systematise it, by allotting to each observer an area of study congenial to his political preferences. Conservatives reported on activities in Conservative committee rooms, meetings, canvassing squads: Labour sympathisers did similarly in Socialist circles. Some degree of objectivity in the reporting was assured by the issue of a schedule of required quantifiable information for each report.

As with the sample of electors, our study of the political organisation fell into two parts—campaign and pre-campaign inquiries.

From October until the beginning of the campaign period, the two members of the survey staff attended as many political meetings, public and private, as they could gain access to. They also interviewed at length rather more than 100 leading political workers in the constituency. Here attention was concentrated on the structure and functions of the organisations, the processes of selecting officers and candidates, the recruitment of members and the uses made of them, the kind and quality of relations with other organisa-tions, including their opponents. So far as time permitted, this phase of the inquiry was extended into the past. Minute books of all three parties were made available to us, and of course local newspaper files and library collections were studied.

Against this background of local information, plans were laid for full and systematic observation of the campaign itself. With the help of an augmented staff, and nearly one hundred volunteers among the students of the London School of Economics and Political Science, it was possible to cover pretty well every activity undertaken in the constituency by each of the three candidates and their supporters. Every public meeting held during the campaign was attended—the larger ones by two or three observers; and records of attendance, speeches, audience reactions and questions were made. Observers worked in committee rooms, and obtained particulars of the party members attending, the systems of inter-party communications, the work done and attitudes expressed about their own leaders, their opponents and the campaign in general. Detailed reports were made on loud-speaker tours, canvassing expeditions, open-air cinema exhibitions and the distribution of literature. Over the three weeks of active campaigning some 300 separate reports were accumulated.

In addition, a daily quota sample of 100 interviews was undertaken to ascertain the extent and impact of listening to the political broadcasts of the previous evening. Similar interviews were conducted on one of the occasions when special leaflets relating to local personalities were distributed by the Conservative Party.

On polling day, some 80 observers were distributed round the polling stations and committee rooms, and, from the sealing of the ballot boxes to the announcement of the count, an hour-by-hour narrative of events throughout the constituency was compiled.

All in all, then, some 150 people have been involved in collecting data on the political attitudes and behaviour of Greenwich citizens during the early months of 1950. In organising these data in the following chapters we have moved, broadly, along two axes of interest: the temporal—from the more remote to the more recent in time; and socio-psychological—from the larger to the smaller group. The first of these represents a traditional and hallowed mode of analysis—obviously past experience conditions present behaviour, and, whether or not the linkage is 'causal' in any sense, the practice is sanctioned by the fact that we all think readily in these genetic terms. Our second axis of interest perhaps requires more justification. Social scientists have tended to study human groups from one of two aspects: they have studied groups in terms of their *products*—whether these be conversations or cathedrals; and they have studied groups in terms of the characteristics of their component members. This latter approach, which lends itself readily to statistical treatment, also lends itself to ambiguity in consequence, for the distinction between a statistical group and a social group is apt to become obscured. If we take all male manual workers of elementary education between the ages of 30 and 49, and show that a very high proportion vote for a Labour Party candidate, it is we rather than they who have grouped individuals in this way. On the other hand, when we find, at the monthly General Management Committee of the Green- wich Labour Party, that a high proportion of the delegates present are male manual workers of elementary education between the ages of 30 and 49, the group is self-defined and we have done no more than apply some common rankings to its members. It is clear that the statistical group of the first case, and the social group of the second, are not un- related; but we can hardly be content with such findings until we know a great deal more about the intermediary social processes by which this relationship, between the statistical group and the social group, comes about. Concern with these intermediary processes—with the living nexus of family groups, work groups, friendship groups and political groups that mediate between the statistical unit and the social ego—is central to this inquiry, and explains why we have sometimes chosen to dwell on data of apparently limited significance at the expense of material of wider political interest.

Chapter Two

THE CONSTITUENCY

T HE borough of Greenwich lies inside the eastern corner of that broken amphitheatre of low hills which encircles south London and falls to the Thames at Putney and Woolwich. Historically no less than physically the constituency takes its shape from the river. If one climbs the slopes leading from the wharves and riverside factories, up past that airy view which Canaletto loved to paint, to the high and windy housing estates of Kidbrooke, one passes through zones of social history as well defined, almost, as geological deposits.

Greenwich children have more opportunity than most to acquire a sense of the past from their lessons, for the neighbourhood is rich with history. It was over a Greenwich pothole that Raleigh spread his cloak so that his Queen could walk dry-footed; and in the park nearby, the eighth Henry conducted many of his amorous adventures. Great ships sailed from the borough's tiny creak: the *Golden Hind*, the *Victory*, the *Discovery*, the *Mayflower*. The greatest of English architects left a lasting vision of human dignity in its Royal Hospital to shame the mean streets that later spread around it; and in a dozen other architectural graces, from St. Alphege's Church to Vanbrugh's folly, the past is kept alive, however faintly, in the minds of Greenwich people.

But if history has given Greenwich so much that makes for corporate pride, history has also eaten its heart out. A whim of William's Mary, that she should be able to walk from her barge to her house between massive colonnades set

29

a hundred feet apart, has added nothing to the nobility of Wren's design, and has made of the Greenwich hospital a too-extensive no-man's-land dividing the borough through its centre. From the viewpoint of community life, the Hospital and the Park, set right in the heart of things, are unfortunately placed; they make communication between one ward and another unnecessarily difficult, and condemn the 85,000 inhabitants of Greenwich to an unfocused, almost centrifugal kind of living. For family entertainment, for much of the week-end shopping, the people go to neighbouring boroughs.

Yet these same scattered neighbourhoods have a strong sense of their own identity. This is in part because the borough has come to incorporate what were, until the flood of Victorian building engulfed them, a number of distinct villages each with an ancient history of its own. St. Nicholas ward, a dozen dismal streets huddling about the historic site of the Deptford dockyards, and belonging to that borough, is still so distinct in spirit from its neighbours that it reminds one more of a mining village than of a London district. Charlton Village, at the other end of the constituency, with its superb Jacobean manor house, its charming church and its homely inn, lends some grace to the raw new housing around, like a Windsor chair in a pre-fab. Around Blackheath there are a few streets and many scattered houses which bring with them the quiet of the eighteenth century, when this was a rural suburb just beginning to be fashionable. It is around such scattered patches of the past that modern Greenwich has grown and oriented itself. Moving about the borough, one often finds that the tracks made by the housewives in the new municipal blocks lead, not to an equally new shopping centre, but to an old and friendly village street.

The development of this pattern has been assisted, not only by the decentralising effects of the Hospital and the Park, but also by the hillside situation. Three miles of railway at the foot of the hills traverse the borough from west to east, and produce a strong 'across the tracks' stratification. Between the railway and the river—owing to the sharp bends here there are four and a half miles of waterfront—is to be found more than 70% of Greenwich industries and 33% of its population. The industries are of the sort that use barge-transport—a power station and a gasworks, constructional engineering, glass, paint, industrial chemicals and cables. They were heavily bombed during the war, and much of the slum property in which their workers were housed has been razed to the ground. To-day 21% of the dwellings in these wards are owned by local authorities—mainly tenement blocks in type. But the characteristic dwelling is still the cheap four-roomed cottage bleakly facing an identical twin on the other side of the street.

In the past the riverside areas were fairly densely populated, but in the last twenty years much of the population has been rehoused. In consequence the wards are now considerably over-represented on the Borough Council—with only 33% of the population they return 53% of the councillors. This gives a decided advantage to the local Laboui Party, which finds most of its support hereabouts. As we shall show in a later chapter, local government affairs influence a party's fortunes in many ways.

When our interviewers went into these riverside wards to gather their samples, they found that 8% of the houses visited were owned by their occupants (compared with 17% for the whole borough), while only 6% were connected by telephone (compared with 15% for the borough). Informants here were slightly easier to contact—they stayed at home more, or were more predictable in their habits; it required fewer visits to a home before finding the person specified. Of 338 names on the interviewers' lists for these wards, 32 proved inaccessible. Some of these were dead, or had moved, or were ill; 12 refused to be interviewed. Comparison of failed interviews in these wards with the failures elsewhere is illuminating:

It will be seen that, although the ratio of obtained to unobtained interviews is much the same for the riverside wards as for the whole borough, there are distinct differences in the reasons for failure. These differences would seem to arise from age differences. The riverside wards contain more elderly people than the borough as a whole; the rehousing of recent years has affected mainly the younger families. The older you are, the less likely you are to move, and the more likely you are to find the novel approaches of the opinion pollster rather disturbing.

Table 2

UNOBTAINED INTERVIEWS COMPARED BY DISTRICTS

Reason for Failure	Riverside Wards	Other Wards	All Wards
	%	%	%
Refused	37	19	24
Moved	28	55	47
Inaccessible	35	26	29

The riverside wards, as we have indicated, present an almost unrelieved aspect of physical poverty. They contain, however, one or two little pockets of prosperity—notably a little colony on the reclaimed marshes where river pilots and other unclassified old salts live in a W. W. Jacobs world of their own. These, and the gasworkers who live in the same area, make a little Conservative-voting enclave in an otherwise solid zone of Socialist sympathisers. Asked what social class they belonged to, 11% of the ward residents called themselves 'middle class', 5% 'lower middle class' and 78% 'working class'. In these wards our poll showed the Conservative vote to be 15%—almost exactly similar to the self-assessed middle-class population.

Above the railway lines lies a band of residential neighbourhoods sufficiently diverse to be treated separately.

The South-East ward, topographically the centre of the constituency, is in fact largely a creation of the railway. It sprawls up the hillside, bounded on one side by the park, to Blackheath, and includes a very heterogeneous population. In the immediate vicinity of the tracks the houses tend to be small and a little pretentious, built in the '70s and '80s with an eye on the Mr. Pooters of the day. Further up the hill there are many large detached houses, where the gardens get bigger and the carriage-drives broader as one approaches Blackheath. A few of these are still inhabited by the prosperous merchants and professional people for whom they were originally built, but for the most part they have been converted into boarding houses and private hotels. Local authorities are responsible for very little building in this area —they own less than 5% of the dwellings—but a good many properties have been requisitioned by the Borough Council, and when these are included the proportion of municipally controlled housing goes up to 17%.

In contrast with the riverside wards, 22% of the houses we visited here were owned by the occupants, and 24% were connected by telephone. There were 169 names on our lists, of whom we were unable to make contact with 15; of these 10 had moved out of the district, and only 2 were refusals. Among the people contacted 31% styled themselves 'middle class', 12% 'lower middle class' and 44% 'working class'. The Conservative vote in this ward as shown by our poll was 44%—again nearly equivalent in numbers to the middle-class population. The Labour vote—at 29%—was well below what might have been expected of those who, living above the tracks, still identified themselves with the working class.

To the east of this ward, but at much the same social and topographical level, is Charlton. We have already spoken of the village which gives coherence and a sense of tradition to this area. The Manor House, which has been acquired by the Borough for a community centre, has until fairly recently been lived in by a family with strong squirearchal traditions, who contrived, if not to keep the modern world at bay, at least to regulate its invasion for longer than most landowners of that kind were able to do. As a result the district boasts two large and beautiful public parks, and a private housing estate that is less offensive than many such Edwardian ventures; in addition, both the L.C.C. and the Borough Council are busy building new blocks of flats on what remains of the family domains. Indeed, if one includes requisitioned property, local authorities now control some 36% of the dwellings in the two polling districts under discussion, where 13% of the borough's population lives.

3   33

In spite of the dominance of council properties in this part of Charlton, however, 19% of the families visited owned their own homes, and a similar percentage of the houses had telephones. We had listed 137 names from this ward, and we obtained all but 18 of them: this representing a higher proportion of failures than in the wards so far dealt with. The refusals and removals were 6 of one and 8 of the other.

The residents of Charlton, perhaps because so many of them have long dwelt under the chastening influence of a manorial regime, have a curious betwixt-and-between uniformity of style; and they reflect this in their self-description, for 13% describe themselves as 'middle class', another 13% as 'lower middle class' and 62% as 'working class'. The Conservative vote, according to our poll, was 23%, the Labour vote 53%.

On the other side of the constituency, west of Greenwich Park, are the South and West wards, built around the old road climbing precipitously up to Blackheath and on to Dover. It was here that Lord Chesterfield wrote his elegant letters, and something of that age still persists in the housefronts and gardens around. The years have added variety of styles, and not always happily; but whatever it is one means by 'character' in a neighbourhood, it is to be found here, where 12% of the Greenwich population live in a tangle of small, climbing streets.

Here again we failed to find 10% of the people on our lists—of 127 names, 9 had moved from the district, and only 1 refused to be interviewed. Oddly enough, although it is a district of small houses, with only 10% of its dwellings owned or requisitioned by local authorities, the percentage of house ownership was low—9%, while telephones were in 10% of the homes. Among these people, 12% style themselves 'middle class', 15% 'lower middle class' and 68% 'working class'. The Conservative vote was, we found, 31%, the Labour vote 47%. It will be noticed that here for the first time the Conservative vote exceeds the percentage of the combined middle classes.

Kidbrooke, forming the southern boundary of the constituency, is by far the largest of the Greenwich wards, and because of its development it needs to be treated as two distinct areas.

The first is that once fashionable suburb of Blackheath which grew around the ancient village and spread, after the coming of the railway, towards Shooters Hill, where dukes and royal exiles lived. The streets in the older parts are broad and lined with stately trees, the houses stand well back from the road and have gardens large enough to accommodate a Conservative Association garden fête; and people prepared to hold such fêtes still live there. In the newer areas the building is more modest, though still substantial; and it goes almost without saying that throughout this district many of the bigger houses have been divided into flats. While there are patches of working-class housing here, hardly any of it is owned by local authorities. Nearly 11% of the Greenwich electors are resident in this area.

The character of the district emerges clearly from the fact that 35% of the houses we visited here were owned by their occupants, and 40% were connected by telephone. With 107 people on our lists, we failed to reach 13; 8 had moved out of the district, 3 refused to be interviewed: 45% of those contacted called themselves 'middle class', 11% 'lower middle class' and 34% called themselves 'working class'. The Conservative vote was 49%, the Labour vote 27%.

The remaining part of Kidbrooke (Kidbrooke 2 in Table 3) has been built up only in the past twenty-five years; previously it had been relatively open country where two large hospitals had settled on account of the salubrious air, and where local industries bought ground for their sports clubs. To-day about half the acreage of the area is still unbuilt-on, and the rest is occupied by housing-projects still in course of development. About half the housing now occupied is owned by local authorities, and the proportion will increase in coming years. Although there are some centres of employment, notably a large transport depot, like most new suburbs initiated during the inter-war years it is socially a very ill-balanced district, badly served with shopping and communal facilities, and with the classes segregated in large uniform 'estates'. Nearly 14% of the Greenwich electorate live here.

Of these people, 21% own the houses they live in, and 17% are accessible by telephone.

With 141 names on our lists for this area, we failed to contact 14; 7 of whom had moved, and only 1 refused to be interviewed. Of those interviewed, 16% called themselves 'middle class', 9% 'lower middle class' and 53% 'working class'. The Conservative vote was, according to our poll, 23%, the Labour vote 53%.

In this very cursory survey of the constituency we have quoted a number of statistics for each area, the significance of which is difficult to grasp until they are arrayed side by side. In the table below, the figures for each area are brought together.

Table 3

COMPARISON OF CERTAIN SOCIAL DATA FOR GREENWICH RESIDENTIAL AREAS

	River-side Wards	Charl-ton	(1) Kid-brooke	(2) Kid-brooke	South West	South East
Percentage of	%	%	%	%	%	%
Borough population	33	13	11	14	12	16
Dwellings owned, L.A.	21	36	negl.	50	10	17
Occupier-owned	8	19	35	21	9	22
Unobtained inter-views	9	13	11	10	10	9
Moved from district	3	4	7	5	7	6
Middle class	11	13	45	16	12	31
Lower middle class	5	13	11	9	15	12
Working class	78	62	34	53	68	44
Official poll returns	81	83·5	86·4	83·4	81·4	84
Membership, both parties	10	15	15	8	10	21
1950 vote, Cons.	15	23	49	23	31	44
Lab.	60	53	27	53	47	29

A fleshless summary of attributes such as this tells us very little about the constituency. It cannot evoke the gritty tenements and ornate pubs beside the river, the flaking stucco of Charlton or the leafy avenues of Blackheath. But it serves to recall, what is too easily forgotten when discussing election statistics, that a 'constituency' is an administrative rather than a social concept. The loose division into districts adopted here is itself somewhat artificial, and a full 'ecological' analysis of the borough would have to deal with many more and much smaller neighbourhood-units, each a district in its own way. But even the crude groupings given above reveal something of the fashion whereby history has worked to produce its social diversities, even within an area of a few square miles.

The table also serves to warn us of some of the analytical difficulties ahead. In general we may expect to find associations between property, class and vote; but it is clear that these categories by no means exhaust the complexities of political behaviour. The very poor and the very rich districts are emphatic in voting against each other's candidates. Yet we find two areas (Charlton and Kidbrooke) with exactly similar distributions of votes and polling records, possessing quite dissimilar social attributes. If there is a cause-effect relationship here, it is no two-way function; we cannot from like effects deduce like causal patterns.

It will be noticed that we have introduced into the table two new sets of statistics—the poll returns for the districts, and the percentage of party membership found in our sample. The poll-returns show close association with home ownership and the strength of the middle-class population in each district, but appear to have little relation to the local intensity of political organisation. Indeed the party membership figures, while varying considerably from area to area, have little apparent relation to any of the other statistics. If we assume that the party organisations spread their energies equally throughout the constituency, then it would seem that they meet with unequal resistance from district to district. Whether or not this is so will emerge in the following chapter.

Chapter Three

LOCAL POLITICAL
ORGANISATION

S CATTERED around the more salubrious districts of
Greenwich are five large, licensed clubs that all owe
their origins to politics. All date from the 1880's, the
period following the great suffrage reforms, when such
establishments were the main instruments by which the rival
parties of the day sought to marshal the support of the newly
enfranchised classes. To-day there is little to choose between
any of the Greenwich clubs, either in the amenities or the
company they offer. In each is a comfortable bar, a billiard
room, a concert room and a lecture hall. In each the membership is exclusively male, and drawn chiefly from the ranks
of small tradesmen, factory supervisors and office workers.
Three of these clubs pay affiliation fees to the Greenwich
Conservative Association and membership is, nominally at
least, conditional upon the acceptance of that party's principles and policy. The other two, while retaining the words
'Liberal' or 'Radical' in their titles, have long ceased to have
political associations.

Any political organisation that hopes to influence large
masses of the electorate needs offices and meeting places
located conveniently to the centres of their activities. This
is the kind of truism that is easily overlooked in the discussion
of political activities, where the hiring of suitable premises
sometimes exposes an organisation to at least negative control by property-owners. In this respect the Greenwich Conservative Association, with its usufruct of three spacious

clubs inherited from the past, enjoys a solid advantage over the three other parties competing for the attention of the borough's electors.

The political history of the division can be inferred from this situation. From 1835 until the introduction of the secret ballot in 1872, Greenwich was a Liberal stronghold. It was indeed one of the few constituencies in the country to have, even before the later extensions of the suffrage, a majority of working-class electors, and returned an almost unbroken succession of radicals. But with the introduction of the secret ballot (Greenwich was the first constituency in the country to use the new polling system) the political fortunes of the constituency changed abruptly. In the seventy years between 1880 and 1950, only four of eighteen elections were won by candidates other than Conservatives.

It would be instructive to undertake a detailed examination of the underlying causes of that abrupt change in the political complexion of Greenwich; but here we can only touch briefly on the organisational aspects. Local legend stresses the alliance between the Conservative candidate of the 70's and 80's, a rich distiller, and the Greenwich publicans (public houses, as Booth remarked disapprovingly in his survey, used to 'line the main roads' of the borough). The introduction of the secret ballot, it is said, made it easier for the working man to ignore the radical sentiments of his mates and accept Conservative bribes. This view gains plausibility from the fact that one Conservative candidate of the period brought a libel suit against his own agent for circulating stories about his bribes. But while such methods may explain the early successes of the Conservative machine, they can scarcely account for their persistence. More important were the changes in social structure produced by the closing of the Deptford dockyard, which forced many workers to leave the borough. But even when these factors are taken into account, the fact remains that the balance of voting strength still lay with the classes who had hitherto voted consistently radical, and whom the extended franchise of 1865 might have been expected to reinforce.

39

The true explanation emerges when one compares the minute books of the two parties of the period, some of which have fortunately survived. The Reform Act of 1867 doubled the Greenwich electorate, and in doing so imposed a very heavy burden of registration on the local organisations. In a sense it may be said that the lowering of property qualifications for the elector had raised them for the candidate. For the great increase in the electorate came without any corresponding improvement in the procedure of registration. The burden of keeping the registers up to date fell on the parties, who each tried to ensure the listing of their own supporters and the exclusion of their opponents. The intensive annual canvasses of the constituency which this procedure required, followed by lengthy legal wrangles before the 'revising barrister', gave great advantage to the party with the longest purse. There is no question but that the Conservatives were the richer of the two factions. In 1890, for example, the Greenwich Liberal Association had a total income of £174, of which £60 was donated by the prospective candidate. For the same year the Charlton Conservative Association, covering only part of the constituency, had an income of £210; none of this came from the sitting member, who contributed only to the Greenwich Association—how much one cannot tell, since the records are not available.

It is very clear that for the thirty years preceding the turn of the century the Greenwich electoral register must have been largely a creation of the Conservative Party.

Throughout these same years the Conservatives had an ideological as well as a financial advantage. For many years there had been no serious differences to disturb the inner harmony of their ranks. The presence of two independent Conservative Associations in one constituency (dating from the days when Greenwich returned two members) was a source of potential strife, and in 1906 it broke into open hostility over the Tariff Reform issue, and led to a temporary loss of the seat. But for the great part of the period the two Associations worked well together. The same can hardly be said of the various factions operating within the single Liberal Association, which was early distracted by the demands of a Labour movement growing rapidly in numbers, articulateness and financial resources. In 1869 the trade unionists of the borough were lending support to a new Advanced Radical Association, which proclaimed as its first object the return to Parliament of 'a thorough working-class representative', and which in 1874 actually put up a socialist candidate to oppose the great Mr. Gladstone. The advanced radicals disappeared as a separate organisation, but in their place came the Greenwich Trades Council, with pretensions to dispose of the union vote and demanding an ever larger voice in the nomination of Liberal candidates. The manufacturers and professional people who were the mainstay of the local Liberal Party found themselves in the position of paying the piper while the trade unions called the tune; and one by one they drifted—the Home Rule crisis of 1886 hastened the process—over to the Conservative camp.

Until 1918 the Greenwich Liberal Association remained an effective if not a thriving body, because there was no other political organisation available to the working man who, without being a socialist, felt that his interests were under-represented in the councils of the nation. But in September of that year a number of representatives of trade unions, co-operative and other societies, met together and formally founded the Greenwich Labour Party.

From the outset this infant party had an astonishingly mature air; its proceedings were brisk, businesslike and informed with a sense of political realities. Nor is this surprising, since most of its new officials had long been active in local politics in other capacities, and three of them until recently had held office in the Liberal Party. It adopted a parliamentary candidate within a few days of its formation—no 'wild man', but a trade union secretary carefully chosen for his blameless liberal past. The effect of this new organisation on the local Liberal machine was immediate and catastrophic. Too disorganised to put up a candidate of their own in the election that followed these events, the Council of the Association formally resolved to support the Labour candidate; whereupon several of the most prominent Liberals in the borough, including some councillors, promptly signed the nomination papers of the Conservative candidate. The Liberal Party never recovered from this disaster. It was never again able to exist continuously, although in three subsequent elections it was re-formed to support a candidate.

Throughout the inter-war years, then, the Greenwich political scene still wore the aspect of a two-party conflict, but there comparison with the past ended. For the Labour Party introduced something quite novel in the form of political organisation.

The Liberal Association had been, the Conservative Association was to remain, essentially an instrument for organising opinions and votes in support of policies formulated by a political *élite*. Their task had been to compete for the ear of the public, by the provision of social amenities if necessary, and to see that where there was sympathy there was also a vote. Both organisations, it is true, sent delegates to national assemblies, the deliberations of which were taken into account in the forming of party policy; but in both cases these assemblies were in a sense graftings on to an established structure, and without decisive influence.

But the Labour Party, in Greenwich as elsewhere, had a quite different pattern. It was primarily a federation of local organisations already long established and retaining their identity and interests; a coalition of pressure-groups seeking direct political expression. Like the other parties it concerned itself with organising votes for an agreed national policy, with the state of the register, and with the provision of social amenities. But unlike them it retained the characteristics of pressure-group structure. It not only provided its leaders with a clear line of communication to the masses; it provided the masses with a clear line of communication to the leaders. Its corporate members demanded full opportunities to express their special interests and have them adopted as policy, and individual members shared the same privilege. The internal process of discussion was as important as the external process of persuasion.

The constitutions of the Labour and Conservative Parties emphasised these differences of origin. Compared with that of its rival, the Conservative constitution is an almost rudimentary document. It does little more than state the conditions of membership, provide for the election of officers and selection of candidates, and indicate the procedure and occasions whereby the association's business shall be conducted. Quite explicitly it leaves internal regulatory detail to an Executive Council which is largely of the co-opted type. It is the constitution of a party which takes its policies and programmes as found, and which anticipates struggles for precedence rather than differences of opinion.

By contrast the Labour Party constitution is an elaborate code minutely governing the relations of the organisation to other organisations, of members to committees, of one committee to another. It determines what business shall be conducted at which meetings, and in what manner. And above all it takes the greatest care to ensure that power is delegated in strict proportion to numbers, so that a minority interest cannot command a majority vote.

Which, with the viewpoint of a simple vote-catching machine, is the more efficient form of organisation? If one takes as the frame of reference the whole thirty years during which these parties have confronted each other, their successes have been remarkably evenly balanced. Excluding the 1918 election, fought when the Labour Party was scarcely four months old, we have eight General Elections to form a basis of comparison, and each party has headed the poll on four occasions. Over the same period, the aggregate of votes cast for each party is surprisingly similar (146,526 votes for Labour candidates; 144,502 for Conservative candidates). From 1918 to 1950, in fact, Greenwich has been a 'barometer' constituency, returning a candidate of Government complexion.[1]

But although there is little difference in the aggregate achievements, there is a great difference in costs as measured by election expense returns. For each vote it has received, the Conservative Association has spent $12\frac{1}{2}d.$, while Labour votes have cost on average only $7\frac{1}{2}d.$ each. In neither case, of course, was this as much as the law permitted them to spend;

[1] It returned a Labour member in 1951 and in 1955.

averaged over the eight elections, the Conservatives have spent 76% of the permitted maximum, while Labour candidates have spent only 54%.

These averages tell us little beyond the fact that the Conservative Party in Greenwich—without reaping any apparent benefit—has had more money at its disposal than the rival organisation. But the ways in which the parties habitually apportion their expenses tell us more.

The heaviest item of any election campaign is likely to be the printing-bills; and here, over the years, the two parties have each spent roughly the same amount in actual money. Of course, since the Labour Party was spending from a smaller total, the *percentage* of its expenses absorbed by printing was higher—62%, compared with the Conservative Party's 46%. But the probability is that both parties have put out roughly equal quantities of leaflets and posters. Similarly, they have both spent about the same amount of money on the hire of meeting-halls and committee rooms. So far as can be judged from the election expense accounts, both parties have paid the same kind and amount of attention to the electorate.

Where the parties do differ greatly in their apportioning of expenses, however, is the salaries paid for clerical assistance during the campaigns. At each election the Conservatives have spent on average £210 for clerical helpers, exclusive of agent's fees, while the Labour Party has spent only £33. This disparity harks back to the characteristics of the party membership. The more active and dominant Conservatives are people trained by circumstance to regard themselves as administrators, who would more willingly pay others to do routine work than undertake it themselves. In the Labour Party the most active and dominant members are usually people who earn their living by routine occupations, and have no status conflicts to overcome in doing party work, however dull.

It is clear from these figures that the Labour Party relies more on voluntary work than the Conservative Association. But voluntary workers have to be trained, if only in the habit of devoting their leisure to party work. And this need, peculiar to the Labour Party, of having always at hand a band of people used to giving up time and energies freely to the cause, helps to emphasise the structural differences between the two leading organisations. Between elections, the Conservatives reduce business meetings to a minimum, and make a point of diluting politics with pleasures. Balls, dinners, whist-drives, garden parties, outings—these are its characteristic occasions, where the chief motive is not direct political indoctrination but goodwill and funds. Apart from such gatherings the members of the ward 'branches' meet infrequently—once a quarter in the most active wards, once a year in others. The burden of organising party activities is carried on by small committees. The Labour Party, on the other hand, tries to multiply the business of administration and to involve every individual member in some aspect of it. Since its inception each ward organisation has met at least once a month, and every member is invited to attend. It is regarded as the hallmark of a 'good' meeting that there shall have been a good deal of discussion—usually of a 'resolution' intended to change or emphasise party policy in regard to some particular issue of national importance. Of course the people who actually attend these meetings regularly amount to a very small proportion of the party's total membership; but even so, there is usually in every ward a band of from ten to fifty people who know their party's structure intimately, who are used to each other's ways, and who have developed the habit of devoting part of their leisure to politics. It is they who make it possible for the Labour Party to dispense with hired help at election times.

Where the structure, functions and demands of parties differ so radically, one would expect to find equally marked differences of membership. Naturally we are in no position to say anything definite about the past membership of the parties, and it would be unwise to assume that there has been no change in recent years. Indeed we shall later describe one such change affecting the Conservative Association. But the strong probability is that any discernible differences found in the membership of the parties in 1949 were even more marked in the inter-war years. The political developments of the post-war years have made the parties more alike rather than less.

In 1949 the Labour Party claimed a total membership in Greenwich of 3,800, while the Conservative Association membership was 2,900. This suggests that rather less than 11% of the electorate was 'organised' under one or other of the two political machines. In our random sample of 1 in 60 of the electorate, then, we would have expected to find 113 people claiming membership. In fact we found 115 such people. This suggests such inordinate accuracy, both in the party lists and in our sample technique, that we hasten to add that the correspondence does not survive more detailed break-downs. According to the Labour Party figures, we should have found 63 of its members in the sample—in fact we found only 57. This is no doubt explained by the fact that most of the people we failed to contact were of the poorer classes, and a few of these might have been Labour Party members too. The discrepancy between the Conservative Association's figures and our own is superficially more alarming. We should have found 48 Conservative members in our panel; we in fact found 58. It seems, in fact, that significantly more people believe they are members of the Conservative Party than that organisation is aware of. But here we have, probably, one effect of the Conservative Party's emphasis on social rather than political organisation. Membership here is, both financially and intellectually, a less exacting business than membership of the Labour Party. The minimum annual subscription to the Association is one shilling, compared with the sixpence a month subscription to the Labour Party. The monthly visit of the Labour Party collector (who receives a small commission for his labours) makes membership of that organisation a more definite engagement than the annual visit, not always carried out, of the Conservative collector. There are probably a number of people in Greenwich, then, who attend Conservative Party whist-drives or garden-parties, and feel committed to it, but who have never formally received a membership card. And the discrepancy between the party's lists and the sample findings is almost certainly due to the relative ambiguity thus introduced into the idea of Conservative Party membership.

What kind of people belong to the parties? As the following

Table 4

SUMMARY OF CHARACTERISTICS OF PARTY MEMBERS

		Conservative %	Labour %	Expected Distribution %
Sex	Male	43	75	46
	Female	57	25	54
Age	21–29	12	19	21
	30–49	40	44	43
	50–64	21	25	21
	over 65	27	12	15
*Socio-economic status**	Av.+	15	2	3
	Av.	52	9	18
	Av.−	28	77	68
	D	5	12	11
School-leaving age	14 and under	36	83	73
	15 and over	64	17	27
Religion	C. of E.	78	65	74
	Non. Con.	9	2	5
	Other	8	17	11
	None	5	16	10
Subjective status	Middle class	57	—	20
	Lower mid.	17	3·5	10
	Working	16	95	64
	Don't know	7	—	5
	No reply	3	1·5	1
Degree of Interest in politics	Very int.	19	33	11
	Moderately	59	46	39
	Little	22	18	45
	Don't know	—	3	5
Number in sample (=100%)		58	57	

* See pp. 102–3.

summary of their characteristics shows, there are striking differences in nearly every respect between Conservative and Labour members.

It will be seen that, among the objective social characteristics, sex, socio-economic status and education distinguish the two groups most clearly. While the sex composition of the Conservatives contains rather more women than the constituency as a whole (and many more than the general level of interest among women would lead one to expect in any political party), the Labour members muster considerably more men. With socio-economic status the differences become acute—Conservative membership is avoided by the poorer sections of the community, as Labour membership is avoided by the wealthier section. And the educational differences suggest that the parents of the two groups had much the same characteristics—at least to the extent that the number of years of schooling depends on parental income.

With age and religion the differences are smaller, but still distinct. Labour members conform more or less to the community pattern in age, while among Conservative members there is a shortage of the youngest, and an abundance of the oldest age-group. So, too, while the Protestant denominations are over-represented in the Conservative Party, minority religionists and the self-styled irreligious are relatively abundant among the Labour members.

The subjective criteria emphasise rather than diminish the objective status differences observed. Where 67% of the Conservatives fell into the upper half of the socio-economic hierarchy, 74% identified themselves with some segment of the middle classes. With Labour members the reverse process took place: although 11% had apparent cause to identify themselves with the middle classes, only 3·5% in fact did so.

The degree of interest in politics revealed by the party members is, clearly, higher than those of the general electorate. But it is interesting to find that a substantial minority of both parties claim little or no interest: there must be other reasons for joining political parties, and these figures give us some indication of their strength. As we might have expected from the differing structures and activities of the two parties, already described, the Labour Party members have on the whole a more intense interest in politics than their rivals. It seems plain enough that an interest in political matters as such plays a smaller part in the Conservative than in the Labour ranks.

Another index to this question of what is implied by party membership is given by the kind and frequency of the activities undertaken. We asked party members three questions on this score: 'Do you hold office at present?'; 'Have you helped the party in the past month, speaking, canvassing, or other work?'; 'Have you attended any party meetings in the past month?' The answers given are tabulated below.

Table 5

ACTIVITIES OF PARTY MEMBERS

	Conservative %	Labour %
Mode of Activity		
Hold office	5	12
Have helped party	9	14
Have attended meetings	26	39
Total (=100%)	58	57

These figures certainly confirm the general picture that membership of the Labour Party is a more exacting commitment than membership of the Conservative Association.

We have already pointed out that, while all offices in the Labour Party are elective, the Executive Council of the Conservative Association may co-opt individual members to itself. It also has the power to nominate the chairmen of sub-committees, who then become *ex officio* members of the Executive Council. It is possible, then, for at least half the Executive Council officers to have power in party affairs without the consent, or even the knowledge, of the body of members. This makes for certain difficulties in comparing the party officers of one body with those of the other: the only valid comparison is between members and officers within each party. But even here the comparison is not valid on all characteristics. Each party, for instance, has a separate section for women and for young people, and each of these sections has its own group of officers. So to some extent the

4   49

sex and age structure of the officer-group is determined by constitutional requirements.

With this caveat we can now introduce the information collected by a series of special interviews with the party officers. When these interviews were undertaken, in October–December 1949, the Labour Party had 110 positions of office to fill in its organisation, and the Conservative Association had 93—to which must be added an indefinite number of committee-offices filled by co-option and nomination. Since it was impracticable to interview everyone holding office, we selected for interview everyone on the two executive committees, and at least one member of each ward committee. In the case of the Conservatives, it was not possible to fulfil this schedule completely; a few of them were unable to find time to be interviewed. But the final panel of interviews obtained with party officers, 32 Conservatives and 45 Labour officers, gives us a sample approximately proportionate to the differences in membership.

We have already pointed out that sex and age characteristics of the officers are affected by organisational needs. When a party decides it needs a youth section or a women's section, it must have young people and women to run it. But there is no obvious reason why organisational needs should be affected by socio-economic status and education. Yet there are interesting differences between party officers and party members on these points. Conservative officers have higher socio-economic status, but a rather lower educational level, than the members—a difference due to a number of 'self-made' businessmen of humble origin among the officers. Labour Party officers are a little better educated, and appreciably higher in status, than their members.

What these tables do not show, but what becomes very obvious to the observer, is that in both parties there is a pronounced tendency for ward officers to be typical, occupationally and socially, of the ward represented. The Conservative Party experiences more difficulty in keeping alive branches at work in the well-defined factory areas than the Labour Party has with its branches in the middle-class areas; nevertheless, in a working-class area you will hear cockney accents from the officers of both parties, and in a middle-class area 'educated' voices are equally typical of both. Whether this is conscious policy or not, the effect is certainly to ensure that party officers are chosen from the kind of people likely to appeal favourably to local residents.

Table 6

SUMMARY OF CHARACTERISTICS OF
PARTY OFFICERS

		Conservative %	*Labour* %
Sex	Male	75	68
	Female	25	32
Age	21–29	13	2
	30–49	44	60
	50–64	28	36
	65+	15	2
Socio-economic Status	Av.+	56	11
	Av.	34	45
	Av.−	9	42
	D	—	2
School-leaving age	14 and under	41	77
	15 and over	59	23
Religion	C. of E.	88	62
	Non Con.	9	17
	Other	1	19
	None	—	2
Total (=100%)		32	45

To what extent are these party officers chosen for their superior political understanding, experience and services to the party? It would be tedious to produce a long list of comparative tables to illustrate these points, but such factors, as might be expected, play a more obvious part in the selection of Labour than of Conservative officers. Labour officers have on average been members of their party longer than Conservative officers. They belong to only slightly more organisations, but hold many more offices in them. They have worked harder for their party, at least in the sense that they have devoted much more time to a wide range of activities. 'Political understanding', of course, is impossible to measure objectively; but there is certainly a good deal more purely political discussion in Labour than in Conservative Party meetings; and at all the meetings we attended, the officers were more likely than members to initiate and lead such discussions.

In both parties the officers have to accept nomination before they can be elected; and in both parties—but conspicuously in the Labour Party—a number of people refuse nomination on the score that they cannot devote enough time to the work. Thus there might be said to be an element of self-selection about both lists. One element that clearly affects willingness to accept office, and even to be active in party work at all, is the family situation of the member. Among married people, if one partner is keenly interested in politics the other is likely to become involved too. So in both parties, where an office is held by a married man, there is a very high probability that his wife has assumed some party responsibilities also. The wife of the Chairman of the Conservative Association was Chairman of the Conservative Women's Section; the wife of the President of the Greenwich Labour Party was an L.C.C. member for the borough. In the ward organisations this pattern is so dominant that it might almost be said that party membership is a family rather than an individual commitment.

In the partisan heat of an election it is not difficult to find a body of people who will carry out the routine chores of the parties. But what inducements can be offered to keep their zeal alive through the doldrums? The problem is in fact not quite so serious as it sounds, for besides parliamentary elections there are elections for the Borough and County Councils to be fought; and in addition there is an occasional by-election in this and neighbouring constituencies, to keep morale high. Yet it is not cynical to suggest that sheer public spirit, animated by an occasional tour of electioneering, does not exhaust the personal incentives required to keep a political organisation in good fettle. And the fact is that the parties, although they do not pay for services in cash, can and do pay in terms of opportunities for social advancement.

'Following our (local) election victories, many more members of the party have been appointed as co-opted members of committees engaged in minor forms of public administration, and have acquitted themselves excellently.' This passage, from the Greenwich Labour Party annual report for 1934, indicates some of the tangible fruits of victory for the party worker. A borough such as Greenwich, with its heritage of old schools, charities and hospitals, provides hundreds of local honorific offices, appointments to which are at the recommendation of the political parties. In addition the parties maintain panels of recommended names from which are chosen Justices of the Peace, members of various official supervisory committees, trustee boards and delegations. Few such appointments do more than pay out-of-pocket expenses, yet they carry great prestige locally, and can even lead, in indirect ways, to occupational advance. These honours are distributed in rough relation to the strength of the parties on the local or County Councils, as our quotation indicates; but since the committee meetings involved usually require attendance during 'working hours', the Conservative Party is able to fill more posts of this nature than its numerical strength would strictly justify. Nevertheless between 100–120 members of the Greenwich Labour Party have been appointed to these various local administrative bodies, together with some 70 or 80 Conservatives. It is a minor form of patronage, but obviously an extensive one; and undoubtedly it is an advantage to the parties to be able to crown with public recognition the devoted services of their workers.

In both organisations a similar procedure is followed for the selection of names to be placed on the panels of eligible persons. Where special qualifications are required or desirable, the small executive bodies make recommendations to the full Councils (or General Management Committee) of the party, who accept or reject the nominations; in other cases, the executive bodies use their discretion as to whether the Councils need be consulted at all. In this, as in other matters, the Labour Party appears to be more meticulously democratic than its opponent: the probability is that honours have to be distributed, not only among the more hard-working members, but among the affiliated organisations as well.

In the selection of candidates for electoral representation, whether for the Borough Council, the London County Council, or for Parliament, the two parties show marked divergencies. The Conservative Party expects candidates for any of these offices to contribute towards their election expenses, although greater stress is laid on this aspect in parliamentary than in local elections. Since it is with the parliamentary candidates that we are concerned in this report, we shall deal with their selection in some detail.

Since 1918 the Greenwich Conservative Association has sponsored five different candidates. Two of these were men with distinguished naval records, becoming to a borough with rich historical associations with the sea. Another was a company director with strong local associations, who represented the constituency on the Borough Council and County Council before being selected as parliamentary candidate. A fourth, director of a firm of brewers, had been a city councillor in Westminster. Of the fifth, who was prospective candidate for a few months only and who retired before his adoption was publicly announced, we have been unable to obtain reliable information.

The formal procedure for selecting a Conservative candidate is simple. A standing selection committee of three officers prepares, from a Central Office panel of names and from other sources, a short list of three nominations. It is impossible to arrive at objective evidence of all the criteria used in selection, but in the minutes of the Executive Committee for March 1938, when the selection of a new candidate was imminent, two desiderata were recorded: one, that preference should be given to a person willing to reside in the constituency, and two, that no person should be selected who was unwilling to offer financial assistance to the party. On that occasion the candidate finally selected met both requirements. Since then, however, the practice of 'selling seats' has been much criticised in Conservative ranks, and a Central Office recommendation has urged constituency Associations to exact no more than £100 per annum from its candidates. In post-war years the Greenwich party has tried to adjust itself to the new style; but, since lavish expenditure on social functions is part of its inherited structure, with only partial success. Thus the candidate selected in 1946 was asked to make only the 'recommended' contribution of £100 per annum. But it was taken for granted that he would continue to contribute to local charities as abundantly as his predecessors. And further, it was 'rumoured' that he would pay at least half of his election expenses and that his wealthy father could be relied on for further donations. A certain ill-will was generated when it emerged that the candidate took the Central Office recommendations seriously.

In the 1938 Minute quoted above a decision is recorded that no mention of promised contributions is to be made when presenting a candidate for adoption to the Council of the party. This at least ensures that, when choosing between two or more persons on a short list, the Council will not be swayed by financial considerations. This arrangement has been followed in the post-war period. At the Council meeting each short-listed person makes a short speech and answers questions, and the voting depends on the impressions created by this brief platform performance. Certainly the Council does not always accept the selection committee's advice. On the latest of these occasions, when the Council was faced with a short list of four (selected from 31 names on the Central Office panel and 3 local nominations) it rejected all of them as unsatisfactory, and combed the lists to find a more suitable candidate among those overlooked by the committee.

The selection of Labour Party candidates proceeds on a rather different basis. Each affiliated society, and each ward committee, has the right to nominate a member for the candidacy; the National Executive Committee of the Labour Party checks the validity of nominations and must give its endorsement to the candidate finally selected. Where the nomination comes from an affiliated society, the grant it is prepared to make towards campaign funds is openly stated.

Of the three candidates sponsored by the Greenwich Labour Party since 1918, two have been sponsored by trade unions, and one by the Royal Arsenal Co-operative Society. The present member, who was selected as prospective candidate in 1932, brought with him an annual R.A.C.S. grant of £150 per annum, with an additional £200 towards election expenses whenever the occasion arose. Thus the Labour Party is probably better served financially by its candidate or his sponsors than is the rival party. Certainly there is every evidence that it pays as much attention to such financial considerations as the Conservatives, and the case of the present incumbent's predecessor illustrates the point neatly. Mr. E. T. Palmer, first adopted as Labour candidate in 1922, was backed by a grant of £100 p.a., with an additional £250 for election expenses, by the Prudential Staff Union. In 1931 this organisation withdrew its support from the Labour candidate, and Mr. Palmer only retained his candidacy by promising to raise an equal sum among his friends. He was unable to do this in the end, and the party was left after an unsuccessful election campaign with debts to that amount. The fact that Mr. Palmer had fought five elections in Greenwich, and won the seat twice, counted for little against his lack of financial resources; he was invited to resign, and was replaced by the more comfortably endowed R.A.C.S. nominee.

This stress on the part played by money in the choice of candidates will serve to bring into sharper focus the real relationship between Parliament and the constituency party. In the constituency, the primary concern is to win votes; and votes cost money. As we shall later demonstrate, although the great majority of electors are quite certain which *party* they intend to vote for, only one in three has, even at the height of an election campaign, any interest in or knowledge of the candidates as *persons*. It would be false to say that the machines are wholly indifferent to personal attributes—a photogenic smile, a quick wit, a headful of plausible arguments are useful. But they can be dispensed with; while the candidate who has any depth of insight or fullness of understanding of socio-political problems is more likely to embarrass than to help his party locally.

The fact is, that a candidate is useful to his local organisation only intermittently. Not even the most scintillating personality can do as much, in the brief span of an election campaign, as a good agent can do in the years between. Thus whatever the needs of Parliament, the constituency needs are sharper; and a candidate rich in talent and experience but poor in backers is unlikely to be selected. This tendency of the machine, to swallow the people who called it into being, is a very real danger to a parliamentary democracy; fortunately the poorer aspirants to power in both parties have so far succeeded in imposing limits to it. What they have not been able to check is the gradual growth in power and prestige of the party agent, largely at the expense of the parliamentary candidate.

Both the major parties in Greenwich employed a full-time salaried agent. The Conservative agent had an annual salary of £650 and was also allowed a paid clerk and the use of a car. The Labour agent, whose salary was £550, had only voluntary clerical assistance and no car. But despite these differences in remuneration, both had comparable political experience and professional training, and both had similar responsibilities for carrying out the instructions of their respective governing bodies. Although the status of an agent is formally the same in both parties, in fact they differ greatly. In the Labour Party, the agent is unlikely to feel or to be at a social disadvantage with the leading party officers, and as a person he will carry equal authority with them. Indeed if, as in Greenwich, he is Secretary to the party as well as agent, he is in an excellent position to impose his views unostentatiously upon his fellow-officers. In the Conservative Party the agent's position is somewhat different. The leading officers of the association are likely to be people of much higher social standing than his own, his salary comes largely from their individual donations, and although they may not treat him like a servant, they are unlikely to cede to him more authority than his contract warrants. Where tensions develop of a kind likely to impair the party's efficiency, the Conservative agent has a harder time than his Labour compeer in retaining control of the situation. Even more important, his electioneering experience is less likely to influence the allocation of party funds.

In the case of the Labour Party it is difficult, in the case of the Conservative Party it is impossible, to say exactly what these funds amount to. The former publishes annually a detailed statement of income and expenditure, but does not include in this the separate, modest accounts of the ward committees. The only source of information about Conservative accounts is the statement given by the party treasurer at the annual general meeting; this is given in totals only, and again does not include the separate, and in this case substantial, accounts of the wards.

The Labour Party accounts for 1949 show a net income, after deduction of costs, of £2,500; to this must be added about £150 retained and used by the ward committees. Of this sum, £644 was collected in contributions from individual members, £210 in affiliation fees, £300 in individual donations and £150 from the Royal Arsenal Co-operative Society parliamentary grant. The remainder derived from the traditional fund-raising activities of a political party—whist-drives, bazaars, dances and raffles, prominent among the latter being a highly organised weekly football pool which earned more than £900.

During this year the heaviest item of expenditure was £1,018 expenses for the bitterly fought Borough and County Council elections. Standing charges—salaries, rates, affiliation fees, repairs, conference fees, etc.—took slightly more than £900. Only the relatively small amount of £350 was spent—apart from the election campaign of course—on public meetings and printed propaganda. This is about £100 less than was spent on similar items the previous year, when the party income was lower by £1,000. In general these accounts, with their heavy items for outings, conferences, summer schools and such—items affecting few people beyond the circle of party members—support the impression of an 'introverted' organisation, as much concerned to elaborate intra-party relations as to impress itself directly on the public.

For the Conservative Association we can give no such detailed figures. We know only that, according to the treasurer's summary, the income for 1949 was £2,322, and the expenditure £1,982, and there was just over £1,000 still in hand. Since the party had fought two election campaigns in that year (in both of which its expenditure was heavier than its opponents'), had purchased a car and an automatic leaflet folding machine and had in addition to the agent and his clerk employed for some months two full-time canvassers, it seems clear that the figure for expenditure is not a total one. The apparent discrepancy may be due to the fact that the individual ward branches collect and disburse fairly large sums in their own right, and present separate accounts to which we have no access. At least two of these wards give lavish parties annually to children and old people for which they make no charge, and all of them give whist-drives, concerts, dances and garden parties that are more attractively presented, better attended and doubtless more remunerative than any such functions organised by the Labour Party.

If, in spite of appearances, the Conservative Association has in fact a smaller income and outlay than the rival party, part of this effect may be due to its advantages of capital equipment. We have already mentioned the three Conservative Clubs with their well-equipped halls where meetings, socials, concerts and whist-drives can be held without charge. In addition the Association rents comfortable offices in the most central district of the constituency—premises which present a marked contrast to the dingy shop in the lower wards where Labour Party business was conducted, against a background roar of tram-cars. It need scarcely be added that the disparity extends to even the smallest items of office equipment.

So far we have said nothing of the two smaller parties, Communist and Liberal, which were operating in Greenwich at the time of our survey. If space permitted, it would be revealing to deal with these at length. For they embody in their structure, in a relatively pure form, features of political organisation which in the major parties can be observed only as admixtures. The Labour and Conservative parties have in common their continuity of existence; they differ mainly in the emphasis they give to their internal and external systems of communication. In the Communist Party we find a political organisation that, while it has continuity of existence, pays hardly any regard to the electorate, qua electorate, at all; while in the Liberal Party we find an organisation that, in Greenwich, came into being simply as an electoral machine for the occasion of the election, and disappeared soon after. One might almost, indeed, study these two parties as 'ideal types', and use the results as norms by which to measure the effects of growth. But since our frame of reference is provided by the election, in which neither of these parties played a dominant part, we can only deal scantily with them here.

The only occasion on which the Communist Party has put up a parliamentary candidate in Greenwich was the 1931 election, when he received 2,000 votes and lost his deposit; it acknowledged at the time that it had only small hopes of winning the seat, and had electioneered mainly to call attention to its existence. In the 1950 election a Communist candidate was standing in an adjacent constituency, and in consequence members of the Greenwich party gave little time to political affairs in their own borough.

Membership of the Greenwich Communist Party seems to have fluctuated considerably over the past twenty years, but it has maintained continuous existence throughout, even if at times it has fallen to the dimensions of a mere study group. To-day it has a total membership of 220. In sharp contrast to the major parties, it is oriented to the factories rather than to the electoral register. Three large factories send delegates (nominated by party members in the factories) to its executive committee, and its main energies are devoted to increasing its influence in trade union branches and the local trades council.

The Greenwich Communists scarcely support the widespread belief that Communists in general are immeasurably more active and dedicated than the members of other parties. Attendance at the private meetings of the party rarely rises above a dozen people, and at the one public meeting organised by Communists during the election campaign—a meeting widely advertised by poster and leaflet—only forty people were present. Nor could it be said that the 220 party members were engaged elsewhere; for on the two occasions when our observers visited the committee room assigned to them in the neighbouring constituency there were eight people at work—two in the room and six out canvassing. It appears in fact that the brunt of the work of the Greenwich Communist Party, whether in union branches, factories or elsewhere, is carried on by a dozen or so ardent souls, who grumble like the officers of other parties at the apathy of their members.

Between the wars, the Greenwich Liberal Association contested the seat on two occasions; each time their poll was in the vicinity of 6,000 votes, and each time they forfeited their deposit. For years at a time the Association was moribund—there were no meetings, no committee, no books. A month or two before each General Election a letter would appear in the local press, signed by an ardent ex-member, announcing grand plans for its revival; but nothing seemed to come of these efforts. In 1945 there was one such attempt, and it led to the compiling of a list of known Liberal sympathisers residing in the borough—there appear to have been some thirty names on it. But again it proved impossible to find officers zealous enough to cement these sympathies, and for the next three or four years the sole active representative of the Association was a young school teacher who held a weekly 'social' for young people in a local community centre, where the room continued to be booked, more by habit than conviction, in the name of the Greenwich Young Liberals' Association.

That the Association should have been revived in Greenwich, and have sponsored a candidate in the 1950 election, seems to have been due to an accident. In 1946 a zealous young man who was Liberal agent in another constituency bought a house in the borough. He had little time to spare then for local politics, but three years later he got a job at Liberal Party headquarters as travelling organiser, charged with the special task of reviving Liberal organisations in a number of constituencies in preparation for the forthcoming election. Living in Greenwich, it was natural for him to begin his organising there. And when in October 1949 the Liberal Party launched a national recruiting week, and our young man found himself in charge of the arrangements, it was natural that the campaign should be launched by a 'Monster Rally' at the Greenwich Town Hall. (It also helped, of course, that Mr. Gladstone had once for a brief, unhappy period, represented the constituency.)

From the viewpoint of the national party, the Rally was not a great success, but in Greenwich itself it attracted some attention, since a pleasant-looking, diffident man was presented to the audience as the prospective Liberal candidate for the constituency. Haltingly, even confusedly (for it was almost his first appearance on a public platform), Mr. Gladstone's successor appealed for support.

Inspirited to find themselves with a candidate, the handful of local Liberals present set to work to build a party to support him. It was uphill work. True, the lively young travelling organiser was now the official agent for Greenwich, but he was also agent for seven other constituencies as well, and could only give an hour or two a day. It was difficult to find places to meet, and when that difficulty was overcome, it was difficult to get people to the meetings. Some thirty or forty people were found who expressed enthusiasm about the Liberal revival, but of the dozen who were prepared to give time to it, only three or four had had any previous experience in the Liberal or any other political party. An attempt was made to set up separate ward organisations, but only one ward was able to muster enough people—nine—at an inaugural meeting to fill the essential offices. Money was needed to provide the kinds of things that will attract people away from their firesides to build a new political community—dances, social evenings, whist-drives, attractive meetings. And little money was available. The candidate was so disappointed with results that he began to reconsider his decision to stand. For the latter half of December the struggling organisation was inactive, while all around its rivals were holding gay and profitable Christmas parties, because the candidate and the National party were not agreed as to the size of their respective contributions to the local campaign funds. Three days after Mr. Attlee anounced the date of the dissolution of Parliament, a financial arrangement was reached, Headquarters would contribute £200, insure the deposit, and pay the agent's salary; the candidate would contribute what he could afford. Unfortunately the settlement came too late, or the election came too early, to allow the association time to build upon it. A band of nineteen people had been found who would give their leisure to the cause; but however valiant their efforts, they could hardly be called an electoral machine. Greenwich, in effect, still had a Liberal candidate without a Liberal Party.

Chapter Four

BACKGROUND TO AN ELECTION

I N the Spring of 1949 the two Greenwich agents emerged from a bout of intense electioneering with much to think about. Labour had carried off the honours—all 3 seats on the County Council, and 21 of the 30 seats on the Borough Council. Their control of municipal politics was still secure. But the Conservatives had no cause for despair. They had missed an L.C.C. seat by only 710 votes, and they had unexpectedly regained two seats in the borough. The rightward swing was perceptible in Greenwich as elsewhere. It needed only to be a little better, a little more energetically organised.

But how? Within the Conservative Party there were two groups with different answers.

One answer was that of the men in control of the party—substantial people with local businesses, who wished to be respected in the community. A party that spends money with éclat, that conducts its political warfare with dignity—such a party would enhance the reputation of its members, and especially of its leaders; as for the masses, they were already disillusioned with socialism, and would rally to leaders who remained sober and steadfast.

The other answer came from a small group of youngsters, who gathered around their prospective parliamentary candidate. Mr. Gilbey had attended one of Lord Woolton's training courses for candidates; he had been taught to attack socialism at all times and without mercy, that there must be no *passive* support for conservatism, that elections are won on doorsteps and not in parties. This appealed to the younger, more impatient men in the party. It also appealed to a number of older people of the professional classes—retired soldiers and sailors—whose interests were national rather than local, and who had a certain contempt for 'business types'.

Had it not been for the unexpected gain of a couple of seats in the Borough Council elections, these two distinct viewpoints might have found some accommodation. But it happened that the newly won ward had been organised on Woolton lines, and the new school of thought was now represented on the Borough Council. A group of three energetic and voluble young men, all new to council work, now had a public platform from which to attack the socialist administration.

Their older colleagues on the Council were not pleased. They tried to impose the customary discipline of the 'Whip', and were outraged when the young men refused to accept it. The new session opened with an ominous quiet while the three young men ransacked the administrative records for scandals.

Meanwhile Mr. Gilbey, their candidate, was spending much time in the constituency, making appearances at every social and political gathering of the party, and inviting his constituents to submit their problems to him at a weekly 'Advice Bureau'. Very few did so at first, but the sympathy and attention they received encouraged others, and by the Autumn the candidate, or his henchmen on the Council, were doing a sizeable business in handling complaints.

The Labour Party observed these events in the opposite camp with a certain restlessness. Mr. Reeves, their own Member, was kept very busy in the House, and since he lived at some distance from Greenwich, was seldom seen in his own constituency. This was a point with which the Conservatives made much play, and the criticism was caught up in Labour circles and tossed back and forth across the floor in Labour committee meetings. In part response to these criticisms Mr. Reeves came in September to spend a whole week in Greenwich, spearheading a highly organised membership drive. He spoke at factory-gate meetings in the lunch

5

hour, and in the evenings from the tailboard of a cinema-van; he spent hours in the company of his agent talking to housewives on their doorsteps. At the end of the week nearly 400 new members had been made.

This was stimulating to party-workers, and for a month or so took their minds off internal problems of policy. But as people drifted back from their seaside holidays and attendance at the ward meetings picked up, three distinct strands of controversy dominated discussion.

The first was the party's nationalisation policy. This had taken a turn of local interest when, at the National Conference in June, it was revealed that the Co-operative Societies were opposed to the Executive's proposals for nationalising industrial assurance. Mr. Reeves, as the Co-op. representative on the Executive, was naturally associated in people's minds with this opposition. Local left-wingers, some of them with much influence in the organisation, found cause for alarm here. Had the Co-operative movement become a Vested Interest, impeding the progress of socialism for its own selfish ends? And was their own Member identifying himself with such dubious attitudes? Perhaps fortunately for Mr. Reeves, the issue faded into the background as another, graver controversy arose.

This, of course, was Devaluation, generally seen throughout the local party as an attack, under American dictation, on the workers' standard of living. In every ward but one this issue was formally debated at some time during the Autumn—occasionally under the guidance of a speaker from the Transport House panel, more often in discussions arising from an anti-Devaluation resolution moved from the floor. Apparent in all this debate was a lively clash of feelings, loyalty to a hard-pressed Labour government contending in the same breasts with the painful sense that old, much revered modes of socialist thinking were either being betrayed or abandoned. The Communist line, that devaluation would be unnecessary if our trade policy were oriented to Russia and the 'Eastern democracies', was much canvassed, but on the whole opinion groped hopefully towards the Commonwealth as a 'third way out'. But as talk of an early election filled the

66

newspapers, loyalty to the party took precedence of all other feeling; criticism of the devaluation measure was muted, and socialist sensibilities looked elsewhere for something to vent their displeasure.

They found it in a newspaper interview given by one of their L.C.C. members. This gentleman, an ardent Catholic as well as socialist, had spent a holiday in Spain, and came back to inform the press that Franco's industrial syndicates had given the Spanish worker more control over his job than his British counterpart possessed.

Such an assault on the anti-fascist sentiments of the left, at a time when so many other sentiments were having to be painfully revised, was intolerable! A cry of 'traitor!' rose from the ranks, a special meeting was called and attended by more than 100 members of the organisation, all hot for the councillor's blood. Only his superior debating skill and finesse prevented the passing of that verdict dreaded by all local politicians—a formal vote of censure.

While the Labour Party were thus engaged, the new young Tory councillors had struck pay-dirt during their diggings into the Borough housing records. They discovered that six of the Labour councillors were living in requisitioned houses and flats, the rents of which were in some cases ludicrously below normal standard. On the surface it had the makings of a first-class scandal—and a scandal, moreover, affecting one of the most popular and prominent Labour members in the Borough. It was with ill-concealed joy that the leader of the trio stood up at an open Council in November and asked for information:

'How many members of this Council are living in requisitioned properties?'

Amidst the uproar that followed, the Labour members in question received at least one crumb of comfort: the Conservative opposition was not of one mind concerning the propriety of this attack. Indeed the Chairman of the Conservative Association, a councillor of many years' standing, rose promptly and publicly to defend his Labour colleagues. He pointed out that the councillors in question had all been bombed out of their original homes, and that they paid rent on the principle, applying to all Council tenants and approved by all councillors, that they should not suffer financially from their misfortune. He further pointed out that not all of them had been councillors at the time they became Council tenants. But though his effort was valiant, it was ineffective. The story of the ex-Mayor of Greenwich who for eight years had lived in a semi-detached villa for 11*s*. 10*d*. a week was raised the next month and reported in the national press.

As politics go, this was a triumph. And only a few weeks before it had been preceded by another triumph which could not help but encourage local Conservatives. At the Annual Conference of the Conservative Party a Greenwich gasworker, speaking in a rank cockney accent, had roused the delegates to an unprecedented show of enthusiasm by assuring them that 'his mates in the Old Kent Road' were fed up with nationalisation. Among that brilliant assembly, this living, visible, audible proof that Disraeli was right in believing all working men are Tories at heart was electrifying: Bob Bulbrook of Greenwich became a national Conservative hero overnight. Gramophone records of his speech were made and distributed by the thousand. His rugged, deep-scored face appeared on hoardings everywhere, saying: 'It's common sense—Vote Conservative.' A film was made of Bob Bulbrook in a Greenwich pub persuading his fellow-proletarians that they had nothing to lose but their chains in voting for Churchill. And he was in constant demand as a speaker wherever a London Conservative Party found itself with a dock-gate or a factory-canteen unmanned.

Between them, Bob Bulbrook and the councillors' requisitioned houses caused a good deal of resentment in Labour ranks. But among the Conservatives they caused even more. The conflict between the old faction and the new was now public, and each side became more intransigent as a result. Attempts by the Conservative Central Office to mediate were unavailing; only the candidate's threat, that if the differences within the party were not overcome he would stand as an 'Independent Conservative', produced a sullen postponement of the 'showdown'. In all this high-level squabbling Bob Bulbrook felt a little neglected, and fearful that, should the balance of power in the Association shift, he would be the least able to consolidate his recent gains in prestige. He worked hard as secretary in his own ward, and he spoke incessantly at meetings in other constituencies. But the fact that he was known to side with the chairman of the party prevented him from being used much in Greenwich.

It was not obvious at the time to what extent the rivalries within the Conservative Party were affecting the working of the electoral machine. The wards continued to work with apparently growing efficiency. In October the revised electoral register was published on which the next election, always imminent, would be fought. Ward secretaries of both camps sat down to study the changes, and sent out their canvassers to secure the sympathies of new electors and the whereabouts of those who had moved. On the surface the Conservative wards tackled the work more systematically. But it was noticeable that they did not spread their energies equally throughout the constituency. The middle-class wards were combed and recombed for stray votes—perhaps with unnecessary thoroughness, since the middle classes can be trusted to take their electoral responsibilities seriously. But the working-class wards were only sporadically attacked, and were left mainly to the paid canvassers. The Labour Party distributed its attentions, not more systematically, but more widely. This was in part a matter of personnel: Labour had more middle-class members willing to canvass their own kind in the 'upper' wards than the Conservatives had proletarians willing to canvass in the 'lower' wards. But also the Labour wards were rather more willing (though never enthusiastic) to help each other than the Conservatives were. Here, indeed, appeared to be the first effect of the split in the Tory ranks. No parallel splits occurred in the ward committees; they took sides as units, and continued to work as efficiently as ever. But co-ordination between ward and ward suffered considerably; and requests for additional canvassers from the thinly manned riverside wards (where the party chairman's prestige was high) were likely to be ignored

at headquarters, where the candidate and his supporters
were gaining control.

Towards the end of the year, as election rumours thick-
ened, there was a spate of fund-raising activities. Both parties
held gala dinners-and-dances; both parties ran Christmas
bazaars. The Conservative occasions were the more im-
pressive and profitable. From the Labour Party dinner came
a surplus large enough to purchase a new duplicating machine; from the Conservative Bazaar a yield sufficient to
purchase a secondhand car. In addition both organisations
issued special appeals for funds. The Conservative candidate
undertook a round of social calls, but in only one case could
we ascertain the result—a cheque for £100 from a local
industrialist. The Labour Party sent a circular to all its
affiliated societies, and received from them cheques for more
than £300. Over and above this the Labour agent had
printed 10,000 facsimiles of tram-car tickets, priced 6*d*., and
bearing the slogan 'Return to Westminster', to be 'sold' as
election souvenirs by the individual members.

Interestingly enough, the agent admitted in private that
in fact he already had funds enough to cover his election
needs. But he thought that, necessary or not, such appeals
were a good thing, because Labour supporters *liked* to believe
their party was poor, and people who were persuaded to
invest sixpence in their vote were the more likely to use it.

From November onwards, the Labour Party wards began
to hold their annual general meetings, and these were the
occasions chosen by the agent to reveal something of his
campaign plans. There were to be mass canvasses, led by
Borough councillors and other bigwigs, in the three or four
wards where membership was weakest: 65,000 envelopes
and labels needed to be addressed before the New Year, and
he wanted each ward to set about their quota at once. Mr.
Reeves, their candidate, would come to live in the constituency during the actual campaign, whenever it should be,
and would stay with one of the councillors. The ward officers
were to look around at once for suitable committee rooms—
at least one in each of the twenty-two 'polling districts'—
for which the rental offered was 25/– for three weeks: it was

desirable, though not essential, that committee rooms should have telephones, and they should not be on Council or requisitioned property. There would be weekly classes, from January onwards, for ward officers, where they would learn the details of the party's election 'system'.

The Conservative Party plans (we were to discover later: at this time they were spoken of only in Executive Committee meetings to which we had no access) were already cut-and-dried at the administrative level. The committee rooms, and the committee room procedure, had been allocated and manned; stencils had been cut for the addressograph machine; the more active members were well instructed in what would be expected of them. What was not yet cut-and-dried was the important question of the issues around which the local campaign was to be built. Here the Executive Committee spoke with many voices. Bob Bulbrook thought that in a mainly working-class constituency it was necessary to concentrate on industrial issues—nationalisation and Conservative relations with the trade unions. The candidate and his young supporters wanted to concentrate on housing, and particularly on the local housing 'scandal'. The chairman of the Association was concerned only to 'keep personalities out of it'. At the moment, at least, the chairman was in a strong position, for as legal owner of the Association's printed monthly news-sheet *For the People*, he could veto any writings therein of which he disapproved. The December issue of this four-page paper carried a front-page article by the candidate on housing which made no mention at all of local housing conditions; and reference to the 'scandal' was confined to four lines at the foot of a half-column of 'Borough Council notes'.

The tension produced by this editorial policy, preceded as it had been on both sides by consultations with legal advisers at the Conservative Central Office, obviously worried this latter organisation. By the end of December it seems to have decided that, although it had no constitutional powers to intervene, it had none the less better take a hand in the situation. Early in January there appeared in Greenwich a charming and efficient ex-military gentleman who, although his home was three counties away, announced that he was prepared to work full-time for the Greenwich Conservative candidate. He came armed with the triple authority of the highest Central Office references, a well-known Scottish name, and a very distinguished military record. Within a day or two of his appearance the date of the dissolution of Parliament was officially announced; and at once this newcomer joined the candidate and his agent as one of the triumvirate directing the Conservative campaign.

A fortnight later, on the evening of January 26th, the formal 'Adoption Meeting' of the Conservative candidate was held in the Greenwich Town Hall. More than 400 members of the party turned up for the occasion—some of them, no doubt, activated by a certain curiosity as to how the officers and candidate would behave. But the platform presented an apparently united front to the audience. The chairman, it is true, was brief and rather colourless in presenting the candidate, but he clapped as heartily as any when the candidate's speech was done. Bob Bulbrook followed in support, and after a colourful performance ('Socialists talk about us exploiting the blacks!! What nonsense . . . Near here there's a great black doctor who can lay a white man on the operating table, cut him open, take out his intestines, put them back and sew him up! That's not exploitation—that's education!') announced his regret that he would be able to spend very little time in the constituency during the coming weeks, since he had promised to give his services where they would be most valuable to the Conservative cause. After him came the agent, announcing something of his campaign plans. The candidate was to speak at 27 indoor meetings, in addition to factory and street meetings. Helpers were needed both for speaking and for canvassing. Too many volunteers were only willing to do office-work. The chairman wound up. He understood some members were worried about the fate of their cars on polling day. He assured owners they were not expected to hand over their cars for indiscriminate use; but they should choose members in whom they had confidence to act as spare drivers, so that the cars could keep running all day. He ended by formally dissolving the constituency party until after the election.

In contrast to the formal, ceremonious occasion devised by the Conservatives, the Labour adoption meeting was a small, intimate and almost hurried affair, tacked on to a meeting of the General Council. It was held at the party headquarters, and the 120 members present had to squeeze themselves uncomfortably into a room capable of seating half that number. Mr. Reeves, the candidate, spoke for twenty minutes, and devoted a good part of his time to apologising for the timidity of the party's election manifesto. 'There have been two sections in our party, the progressives— they're the ones in a hurry to get things done—and the consolidators, who think our course to socialism should be slower. Well, this time a middle course has been chosen between the two.' He was followed by the Trustees of the Election Fund, who told the members they still had to find £200. And these by the agent, who told the meeting that there would be 21 committee rooms opened in the borough, manned by 350 volunteers. He'd obtained 4 large poster-sites, and was printing 2,000 small posters with which to cover the smaller sites. There were 7,000 window cards available with the candidate's name, and he wanted every one of them to show. There would be 9 indoor meetings only, but a prominent speaker at each of them. His speech, with its precise figures and general air of competence, was warmly received; but—again in contrast to the Conservative meeting —there was a good deal of discussion between platform and audience about particular points, some of it heated. Comparing the audiences of the two meetings—Conservative and Labour—one could not escape the impression that here everyone was personally *involved* in the election campaigning, while at the other and larger meeting the audience were content to give their applause and their pence, and leave the rest to their officers.

A notable feature of the Labour meeting was the warm affection and admiration of the members, not so much for their candidate as for their agent. At the Liberal adoption meeting, held a few days later in a local school hall, this particular feature was even more accentuated. The Liberal candidate had had a trying time and was starting a head cold; his speech, an inexpert rehash of the pamphlet *50 Things A Liberal Government Would Do*, lacked enthusiasm and roused none. But most of the 40 middle-aged people assembled in the audience had heard of the prodigious feats of the young Liberal agent, who was working eighteen hours a day in his efforts to save the deposits of eight different candidates. Already legends were springing up about him—that he smoked eighty cigarettes a day, that he rarely went to bed. He was rapidly becoming a local hero. So that when he told the meeting briefly that his one committee-room would be open until midnight each evening, and he would need all their help, there was a quite remarkable burst of applause. And when, further, he spoke of the handicaps under which he worked for lack of funds, and called for donations there and then, a total of £151 15s. was contributed within fifteen minutes. True, £75 of this amount was the candidate's contribution; none the less the little audience seemed startled by its own enthusiasm. Like the others the meeting ended with the Liberal Association, which could scarcely yet be said to have existed, formally dissolving itself until the election results were known.

Chapter Five

THE LOCAL CAMPAIGN

I N this chapter we shall confine ourselves to a description of the election campaign as seen in the constituency. The subject-matter will be a series of more or less public events, of the kind that were, or might have been, reported in the local press. Any attempt to assess their effect on the electors of Greenwich will be deferred to subsequent chapters.

Before entering into this narrative it will be useful to attempt some preliminary distinctions. The election campaign as conducted by party national headquarters, and the election campaign as conducted by the constituency agent, have rather different functions, and it is well to bear these differences in mind. The function of the national campaign seems to be to create a favourable 'public image' of the party —a distinct, unitary view of its record, policies, aims and leaders. Whether he be Liberal, Labour or Conservative, the party manager at the centre hopes that wherever the name of his organisation is heard there shall follow, as day follows night, a chain of affective associations—honourable record, wise policies, just aims, powerful leaders. Of course he will never be allowed to build up such an image undisturbed; his opponents will constantly be trying to discredit his efforts. And the very dynamics which have produced the party will tend to emphasise one aspect of the image rather than another. The history of the parties suggests that this tendency to emphasise one salient feature of the public image leads to a weakening of other aspects. In this century the Liberal Party, and after it the Labour Party, has relied on the appeal of promising policies; and since in the nature of things performance can rarely match promise, they have found themselves with vulnerable records of office. The Conservative Party has seemed to rely on the powerful personalities of its leaders—and the permanent 'sentiments' of Conservatism. But however this may be, it seems probable that the views which the general public entertains of the political parties consist of two distinct stereotypes—one 'good', and promulgated by the party itself, the other 'bad', and promulgated by its enemies. In his efforts to ensure that his own stereotype dominates, the party manager seeks to standardise its presentation and universalise its distribution. He tries to have the same arguments, the same pledges, the same criticisms presented on every platform throughout the country. And his powers in this respect have been enormously enhanced in the last thirty years by the development of radio and films.

Between elections, relations between national headquarters and local machines are primarily those of source and sounding-board. In Greenwich, at least, the local parties devote little energy to the direct initiation of political propaganda; their function is to discover those among the electorate who are receptive to the stream of messages emanating from headquarters, to sensitise them further, and to send them back to their homes, clubs and factories as more efficient amplifiers of the party image.

But with the onset of an election the function of the local organisation changes abruptly, and there is little the national headquarters can do to ensure that it performs its new role —except by issuing a perpetual stream of advice and admonition to its agents. This change of function hinges on a simple legal fact—that no indication of a candidate's political affiliation is allowed to appear on the ballot paper. Once inside the polling booth, the elector is faced only with an alphabetically listed group of names.

The constitutional fiction, that the elector is voting for an individual and not a party, thus imposes on the election agent as his paramount duty, the attempt to establish in every constituent's mind a firm, unambiguous association between his candidate's name and party. What the party's aims, record and policies are he can largely leave at this time to the national press, radio and cinema. If he and his party have done their work well between times, the great majority of his constituents will already have taken political sides. For the local agent the election campaign is simply a period during which, with financial resources strictly limited by law and human resources limited by the success of his past endeavours, he must contrive that name-and-party, inseparably linked, are repeated in every form and in every home.

This elementary fact dictates the kind of activities which dominate the local scene during an election. There must be as many posters as possible in all the main roads of the constituency, endlessly repeating name and party. The candidate himself must be seen, in as memorable circumstances as possible, by every constituent. Leaflets bearing his name must penetrate every home. And as many people as can be persuaded to do so must go systematically from door to door repeating the essential syllables: *Reeves . . . Labour*; *Gilbey . . . Conservative*; *Dale . . . Liberal*.

In a constituency of 61,198 electors, and with a legal maximum expenditure of £832, it is clear that the success of an agent's campaign will depend largely on the amount of voluntary help he can muster for the occasion. If his attack is to be both varied and well executed, he will need above all a number of experienced, capable administrators who can give full time to the work and relieve him of whole areas of administrative details. How did our three parties fare in this respect?

Apart from the candidate, agent and secretary, the Conservative headquarters in Greenwich enjoyed the full-time assistance of two ex-military gentlemen—a brigadier and a major—a young law student, and a lady who organised the preparation and dispatch of campaign literature. All these people worked for twelve or more hours a day throughout the campaign.

The Labour headquarters were less generously staffed. Apart from the agent, the candidate and his wife, the only full-time workers were an old-age pensioner and one woman.

On the other hand there were a good number of people—including 21 borough councillors—who managed to take more or less time off from their normal work and to whom the agent was able to delegate a good deal of his work. In this respect the Conservatives were less well served. We could count only a dozen people who were spending more than four hours a day in what may be called an 'executive' capacity—although there were in both parties a good many housewives prepared to spend afternoons and evenings doing routine work, and we found at least two instances where local employers who were members of the Conservative Party released a clerk from their offices to help with the campaign work.

The Liberal agent had scarcely any need to make distinctions between executive and other help. In his one committee room (which also served as headquarters for seven other candidates) there were always too few workers to permit any separation of functions. A dozen ardent souls—schoolteachers, minor civil servants, all members of the professional classes—devoted most of their leisure to the campaign, and co-opted their families and their friends where possible.

These, then, were the lieutenants of the election—the people who ran committee rooms, saw that the agent's instructions were carried out, and reported back to him. In all parties they were for the most part middle-aged men, of higher social standing than the mass of party members, and used to taking a leading role in community affairs.

But lieutenants need troops, and it was here that the greatest differences between the parties were to be found. Throughout the campaign there were about 120 Labour Party members who devoted pretty well all their leisure time to the election, and there were twice as many others who helped for two or three evenings a week. On two or three occasions when our observers chanced to be present in Labour committee rooms, strangers walked in off the streets and asked if they could help: this was never once observed in the Conservative committee rooms. It is more difficult to estimate the Conservative resources, since their system of communications required much less banding together at central points where it was possible for our observers to count them; but it may be doubted if, through the three weeks of campaigning, as many as 100 local party members gave time to electioneering. On the other hand the superior equipment of the Conservatives—there were four cars constantly at the disposal of the headquarters staff, compared with one at Labour headquarters—made their helpers more efficient in some respects.

Two extraneous circumstances helped to blur over, locally, the question of when precisely the campaign may be said to have started. The fact that a general election had been expected for some months past had keyed up both major parties to a state of preparedness and impatience where the agents found it difficult to hold their more zealous workers in check. Yet on this occasion it was more than usually necessary for them to do so. Uncertainty about what precisely constituted an 'election expense' had been introduced by the debate surrounding 'Mr. Cube' and other anti-nationalisation advertising. The official date for the opening of the campaign might be supposed to be set by the dissolution on February 3rd—a date reinforced by the fact that the series of election broadcasts began the following evening. But both local parties found cogent reasons for beginning a week earlier.

Among these reasons was the problem of the monthly broadsheets which both parties published, and which were normally distributed during the first week in each month. The Labour *Greenwich Citizen* (cost and space shared with the Royal Arsenal Co-operative Society) had an edition of 8,000; the Conservative *For the People*, a smaller and less expensive production, had an edition of 5,000. Would the February issues of these papers count as election expenditure? When the date of the election first became known, both agents decided to take a risk, and produce their issues a week earlier than usual—before the dissolution, in fact. But among the Conservatives dissension broke out again about whether the 'facts' of the local housing 'scandal' were to be published; this time the dispute was *à l'outrance*, and the chairman suppressed the issue altogether. So, in the event, it was only the Labour paper that was published; and finding himself alone in the field, the Labour agent decided to include its costs—£8—in his candidate's accounts. Copies of this paper were being circulated during the last week in January.

But for the majority of Greenwich electors the campaign began on January 30th. On the morning of that day, a Monday, rows of yellow-and-black fly-posters repeating the words . . . *Reeves* . . . *Labour* . . . *Reeves* . . . *Labour* . . . appeared on most of the bomb-site walls in Lower Greenwich. Liberal fly-posters appeared a day or two later. Conservative fly-posting was strangely late in starting. Although there were four or five large 16-sheet posters of national type on the local hoardings, the Conservative candidate's name was still rarely to be seen a week after the others had become familiar sights. The Labour agent was uneasy, believing that his opponents were holding their fire deliberately to discourage the enthusiasm of his own workers. But he was mistaken: there had been a simple delay in printing.

But if the Labour agent dressed the scene, the Conservative candidate was first on the stage. While Mr. Reeves was still in process of moving with his family into the constituency, Mr. Gilbey—also on January 30th—held the first of his public meetings. Here again circumstances enforced an early start. A metropolitan Conservative agent is almost forced to adopt a different plan regarding public meetings from his Labour opponent. Most of his party's leaders stand for rural constituencies, and cannot, as readily as Labour leaders, appear briefly in three or four urban constituencies on a single evening. It is difficult to attract large crowds without a big name for bait, and since the Greenwich Conservatives had failed to secure more than one minor celebrity, the idea was adopted instead of holding a great many small meetings, at least one in each of the 22 polling districts. This strenuous schedule required an early start; and the Conservative candidate had already held 11 such meetings by the time Mr. Reeves faced his first indoor audience of the campaign. On this occasion, and only one other, he was the main speaker; but for the rest of the period he was rather overshadowed by the celebrities his agent had managed to secure. Herbert Morrison, Edith Summerskill, George Isaacs and others all appeared (some very briefly) on Greenwich platforms, and attracted sizeable audiences. Thus although the Labour agent arranged only 11 meetings to the Conservatives' 27, the gross audiences reached were of much the same size. According to our observers' estimates, both candidates addressed some 2,200 people in this way.

It is possible that the Conservative audiences might have been larger had the meetings been publicised more efficiently. One meeting had to be abandoned because only 5 people turned up. On another occasion, an observer found that leaflets, intended to be distributed in the vicinity the day prior to one meeting, had not been given out three days later (perhaps in consequence, the audience on this occasion was 21).

It would have been interesting to be able to compare in detail the content of the speeches delivered from local platforms with that of, say, the radio speeches of the party leaders; unfortunately we cannot. But from the summaries provided by our observers it is clear that, if the full distance between the Statesman and the Agitator was never completely revealed, many of the local speakers did their best to extend the lower limits. The less formal the occasion, and the less likely the speaker was to attract the attention of the press, the less measured and responsible was his utterance. Thus visiting celebrities used facts and figures in their arguments with much regard for accuracy—often pausing in their speeches to consult the slips of paper provided by their secretaries. The candidates, repeating much the same speeches from meeting to meeting, and relying much more on their memories, were demonstrably less meticulous. And the local supporting speakers (both parties had a councillor or two on the platform at most meetings) all too frequently allowed their partisan zeal to get the better of their respect for facts. During an election campaign there is a perhaps inevitable tendency to extend the concept of causation until all human good and evil becomes consequent upon political action; and the Conservative councillor who declared that 'the rising suicide-rate among old age pensioners is only one example of what happens under a socialist government', or the Labour councillor who claimed that 'nationalisation of the mines has caused a great reduction in the accident-rates', provided only the more extreme examples of a general tendency. Both sides laboured equally hard to prove that whatever was unpleasing in past or present was the fault of their political opponents, and whatever was pleasing was due to themselves. On the whole the local speeches followed closely the policies put forward in the party manifestos, and dealt with local affairs only by way of illustration. Thus Conservative attacks on the nationalisation and housing policies of the late government were enlivened by reference to the local gas industry and housing shortage; while Labour claims to have abolished unemployment were frequently supported by reference to Thames shipping. But there were on both sides some interesting redistributions of emphasis to meet local interests. The Conservative speakers devoted more of their time than might have been expected to spelling out the implications of the paragraphs in *The Right Road* regarding relations with the trade unions. They talked at great length about 'the right to strike' that unionists would enjoy once more under a Conservative Government, and about the growing gap between the workers and the union bosses with their eyes on the princely salaries of the national boards. Conversely, the Labour speakers spent a lot of their time (particularly after Mr. Churchill's 'Let me Talk to Stalin' speech on the 14th) decrying the Conservative leader's influence abroad. Indeed, during the final ten days of the campaign, one of the principal speakers at every Labour meeting was a young American student, presented as 'a voice from America', who told his audiences in a rich Middle West accent that they must not believe the 'Tory lies' to the effect that the American people wanted Churchill to win, since the contrary was true—the American worker wanted a Labour victory to strengthen his hand in dealing with reactionaries at home.

One quite consistent difference between the speeches of the two parties was the extent to which they used—or were able to use—the names of prominent politicians as symbols. For the Conservatives, and doubtless for their audiences as well, the Labour Party was an assemblage of many well-known names, each with a rich aura of associations. We asked our observers to record every occasion in the speeches that a specific personality was mentioned; and while Conservatives during the campaign made mention of at least fourteen living Labour leaders, the Labour speakers mentioned by name only four of the opposition leaders, with Mr. Churchill getting as many mentions as the other three put together. It goes without saying that each party mentioned its opponents only to denigrate them; the interesting point is that names sprang readily to Conservative lips, but not to Socialist ones. We may legitimately infer from this that the electorate had only a hazy idea of Conservative leadership outside the three figures of Churchill, Woolton and Eden; and if there is anything to the proverb which says that we fear the devil we know less than the devil we don't, we can see here the political disadvantages that accrue to a party that has spent five years in the wilderness and the preceding five overshadowed by its own effulgent leader.

The constituency meetings are the chief opportunity provided for the electorate to question the candidates and bring directly to their attention the problems pressing hardest upon it. In this the Conservative system of many small meetings, with the candidate the chief attraction, served the electorate better than the large and star-bedecked meetings of the Labour Party, where the succession of speakers left little time for questions. In fact, our observers report that 149 questions from the audience were dealt with on Conservative platforms, and 45 on Labour platforms. These audiences consisted almost entirely of the party 'opinion leaders', who are also the people who read their newspapers and pamphlets most attentively. Their questions cannot then be taken as the spontaneous expression of the preoccupations of the entire community. Many of them—as the wording makes clear—were designed either to embarrass the candidates or to help them score additional points. Yet other questions came from obviously inspired sources—Communists, Catholics, anti-vaccination leagues and other pressure groups had their emissaries at the meetings. But although it is doubtful if one question in five was the product of a genuine desire to seek enlightenment, the distribution of these questions by subject is interesting:

Table 7

THEMES OF QUESTIONS ASKED AT
CONSTITUENCY MEETINGS

Themes	*Percentage of all Questions asked* %
Housing	16
Nationalisation	14
Social services	14
Foreign policy	11
Unemployment	11
Wages, trade union matters	11
Taxation	5
Conscription	2
Miscellaneous	16
Total (=100%)	(194)

In general, heckling was observed only at the bigger meetings—and this meant that Labour speakers came in for the lion's share of it. But on the two or three occasions when Conservative audiences passed the 150 mark the proceedings were no less lively than those elsewhere. It was very noticeable that, although audiences were in general middle-aged, the heckling, and most of the questioning, was done by younger people.

In addition to these public meetings there was the usual crop of semi-private gatherings to which candidates came by invitation—invitations, needless to say, which the agents sometimes engineered. The Labour candidate spent a wary evening with the Greenwich Trades Council—an organ on which Communist representation was strong. In exchange for a pious hope that trade would be increased with the 'Eastern democracies' he received a promise from the trade union delegates present that their local branches would support him. Mr. Reeves also addressed an afternoon gathering of the Co-operative Women's Guild, and the senior class of a grammar school. Mr. Gilbey addressed the same class, as well as the local branches of the Catholic Parents' Association and the Licensed Victuallers' Association. Both candidates appeared, separately, in the canteen of a local shipyard, and together in a Brains Trust organised by the local churches.

The Liberal candidate held three public meetings during the campaign, with audiences declining progressively from 45 to 31. A collection was taken at the second of these meetings and produced a total donation of one single coin.

More electors were reached, if more fugitively, by means of open-air meetings and loud-speaker tours. Open-air meetings had formed an important part of the Labour agent's plans, and he hired a large van and equipped it with a microphone for use as a mobile platform. But two attempts to hold evening meetings at street corners, which engaged six of the most able members of the party for three or four hours with an audience smaller than each might have reached separately on a door-to-door canvass, proved very discouraging, and were never repeated. Much more successful were the lunch-hour meetings at factory gates—and, incidentally, more successful than Conservative attempts to engage the same audiences. But by far the most effective use of outdoor speakers was made by the Labour agent in the courtyards of Council flats, in conjunction with squads of canvassers. True, the immediate audience consisted only of children; but while voices were pitched to boom through the furthest windows, canvassers ranged the corridors with leaflets and appeals for funds; and the flush of window-cards that appeared on display after each such visitation testified to the success of such methods.

The Conservative agent did nothing quite in this line. Morning and afternoon the candidate, accompanied by two or three articulate supporters, toured the main roads of the borough in a car equipped with amplifier. Mornings, the housewives in the shopping areas; afternoons, the side streets in the vicinity of the evening's meeting; early evening, the queues at bus and tram stops. On these tours the car would stop for five minutes in one place, and the candidate, after being duly announced, would deliver a three-minute talk on housing or the cost-of-living or the virtues of free enterprise. There would usually be 30 or 40 people within earshot, half a dozen of whom would pause and listen till the car moved on.

Both parties had cinema vans in the constituency for two days. The Conservative van showed a film in which Bob Bulbrook talked tellingly with people in a Greenwich pub, but surprisingly enough no attempt was made to exploit this local association.

None of the Greenwich candidates was an outstanding personality in the gossip column sense of the phrase. They were alike remarkable only for their modesty, their lack of flamboyance, and the patent sincerity with which they expounded their diverse views. Differences of experience were apparent in their platform performances. Mr. Reeves, with five years of Parliament, several years of local government and thirty years of political agitation behind him, had a competence which his rivals lacked. Mr. Gilbey, who had nursed the constituency for three years and had been through a short training course for fledgling politicians, was a little awkward in the early days of the campaign but improved daily. And Mr. Dale, the Liberal, with no previous electioneering or political experience at all, was so manifestly unused to speaking in public that he won the immediate compassion if not the confidence of his audiences. But they all campaigned without apparent zest, like men overawed and overpowered by the forces they had unleashed; and often the fuss and fury surrounding their public appearances seemed to embarrass them. Gladstone is said to have held a crowd of 10,000 people on Blackheath, standing spellbound in the rain while he recited Homer to them. The circumstances are inconceivable in which any of our three candidates could have held an audience of any size in the rain. They were none of them spellbinders, or masters of thought, or more than ordinarily memorable. Yet their agents had to ensure that their names and affiliations were stamped clearly on the memory of each elector. The meetings, heralded by leaflet and poster, helped. The house-to-house visits with which they each filled their otherwise unemployed hours helped also. Yet for all their labours it is doubtful if any one of the three was seen and heard in person, however fleetingly, by more than one-third of his constituents. To assail with key words the eyes and ears of the other two-thirds—this above all was the task of the committee rooms and their bands of willing helpers.

On February 4th the Labour agent opened 9 committee rooms, 1 in each ward; and within the next fortnight 14 more were brought into use. The Conservatives mustered only 16 committee rooms in all—in the most strongly Labour section of the riverside wards they maintained a single room 'for enquiries only'. But in addition they had one sizeable hall where all the chores of sorting, folding, addressing and distributing literature were centralised. The Liberal agent managed with a single committee room (his domestic parlour) throughout the campaign.

The basic function of the committee rooms was to stimulate and organise canvassing. Here were kept the 'marked' registers for the area, and here the officer in charge tried to ensure that a visit was paid to each listed elector. This ideal was nowhere achieved. Few ordinary party members like canvassing, and to persuade them it is necessary to conjure up a spirit of derring-do. And even the best and readiest canvassers are often reluctant to persist beyond the first person to answer the door of a house; it often happens that the reply: "We're all Conservative in this house" by one person is accepted by the canvasser as a reliable guide to the opinions of a dozen people. Observers who accompanied canvassing teams of all parties found that there was great variation in the diligence of individual canvassers, particularly during the early days of the campaign; as the election drew nearer and householders were more ready to express their intentions, the quality of the canvass improved.

Much of the Conservative canvassing was done by a small band of young men and women who formed the nucleus of the 'Greenwich Young Conservatives'. Youth, as a distinct element, played a much more conspicuous part in Conservative than in Labour campaign activities, and it was these Young Conservatives who provided whatever gaiety and boisterousness was found in Greenwich during the campaign period. They threw themselves into electioneering as into a rugger-scrum or a student rag. They heckled vigorously at Labour meetings, they delivered leaflets at all hours, and above all they went canvassing in streets where most Conservatives were loath to penetrate. But apart from these young people there was a lack of canvassers in the Conservative ranks. In part this was the penalty of concentrating between elections on social rather than on political activities; there were more women than men at the agent's disposal, and women not only tend to be unwilling to canvass, but more unwilling still to venture into strange territory. But in some degree also the Conservatives were hampered by their own efficiency. They had been canvassing fairly systematically throughout the year, with paid and unpaid help. Their 'street-leaders' believed it necessary only to canvass new arrivals and report the new addresses of removals; and their officers were telling our observers (and each other) at the very beginning of the campaign that they had 'finished canvassing'. Thus in many areas the officers felt no need to undertake another campaign canvass. As a result much of their tactical information was unreliable and in addition they minimised their opportunities for advertising their candidate's name. One got the impression that some of the Conservative officers, capable and efficient as they were, did not really understand the purposes of an election canvass.

In the Labour committee rooms the supply of canvassers was much more plentiful; the Labour agent's pre-campaign boast, that he could expect some 350 active volunteers to be at his disposal, proved to be a reasonable estimate. By the end of the first fortnight one or two of the smaller wards had completed their registers and were helping neighbouring wards to complete theirs. There was probably no evening of the twenty days' active electioneering when there were not 50 Labour supporters out 'on the knocker'. The Conservatives score was rarely higher than 20—although, unlike Labour, they could sometimes muster a dozen lady canvassers in the afternoons as well.

Both parties used much the same canvassing procedure—the anxiously respectful approach, the stressing of the candidate's name, the pressing of leaflets into reluctant hands, the hopeful suggestion that a window-card will be displayed. That a visible token of his call should appear in the front window with his candidate's name on it was the chief reward of the good canvasser. A good display of cards of one colour in a street discourages opposition canvassers, and serves other, more positive functions as well. It has been suggested by some political commentators that the window-card is a potentially dangerous instrument of mass coercion. Perhaps more important is the simple, obvious function of reminding casual passers-by that an election is imminent, that it is quite respectable to have views about it, and that the local candidates' names are such-and-such. These are public functions, and during our inquiries we received hints of private ones too; for some electors the window-bill was a protective device, for many others it provided a sense of direct participation in important affairs. A rough, random count made in the last days of the campaign suggests that window-cards were displayed in 1 home in 5. Apart from one or two blocks of council flats, where every other window sported a Labour card, the heaviest concentration was in the South-East ward, heavily canvassed by both parties. Labour cards outnumbered Conservative by about 3 to 1—a reflection, not of the real distribution of forces, but of the amount of canvassing done.

Of the overall accuracy of the two parties' canvasses it is difficult to attempt an estimate, but in the middle of the campaign we were given the so-called 'final canvass' figures for two polling districts, one set of figures from each party. In the district covered by the Conservative figures, no further canvassing was undertaken. In a district with just under 5,000 electors, the Conservative canvassers had found 37% of the register intending to vote Conservative, and 40% intending to vote Labour. The remainder were 'doubtfuls'. In our

December interviews we found 25% of the voters in this district intending to vote Conservative, and 49% intending to vote Labour. (The final interview showed 31% voting Conservative, and 51% voting Labour.) Thus where an accurate canvass should have revealed a minimum of 15% points' advantage to Labour, the Conservative canvass indicated only 3 points. It must be added that this was probably the most extensively and accurately canvassed district in the constituency, so far as the Conservative party was concerned. The Labour canvass of the second district did not claim to be quite complete—'There's a few houses we haven't done yet, where we couldn't get an answer'— and was in fact only 80% completed. But at that stage the canvass results showed a 60% vote for Labour, a 25% vote for the Conservatives, and the rest 'doubtfuls'. These figures were wildly different from those obtained by our sample interviews, where the December panel indicated a 47% vote for Conservatives, and a 39% vote for Labour, falling by polling day to 45% and 31% respectively. Thus the Labour canvassers overestimated their support even more grossly than the Conservative canvassers. In both cases, it seems clear, the partiality of the canvassers, and the tendency of the canvassed to say they are voting for the canvasser's party so that they can shut the door again and get back to the fire, makes the information obtained highly unreliable; and if information were the main purpose of the canvass, the energies devoted to it would be misapplied.

At no time during the campaign did the Labour agent betray any uneasiness either as to the extent or the results of his canvass. But on February 11th the Brigadier (as the Central Office emissary was now called by his colleagues) made a tour of the Conservative committee rooms and, dismayed by what he found, spent a frantic hour telephoning and telegraphing members of the executive committee. A meeting followed the next evening, at which 16 people were present. A notable lack of liaison between headquarters and outposts was reported. Some committee rooms had run out of literature, and no replenishments had been provided. One or two districts had finished their canvass, but had not reported the fact so that the workers freed could be directed elsewhere. There was much mutual recrimination, and some hard words for the candidate. The agent's choice of posters was condemned, and the name on the window-cards was said to be illegible at any distance. It was decided that a daily visit should be paid by the candidate to each committee room, and that an effort should be made to obtain 20 outside canvassers from Central Office. (While we know that this appeal to Central Office did not go unheard, we were unable to discover exactly how many outside helpers were in fact provided.)

We have said nothing in this account of Liberal canvassing efforts. There was, in fact, very little. For the first fortnight of the campaign nearly every known Liberal in Greenwich was drafted on to the work of addressing 38,000 envelopes for the posting-off of election addresses. After that the election addresses themselves had to be folded and put into the envelopes. This in itself was almost more work than the little band of zealots could manage in the time available, and only 3 Liberal canvassing expeditions, involving 12 man-hours of work in all, are known to us. Eight promises of votes were obtained, and one offer of help.

One general remark on the subject of canvassing needs to be made before we pass on to other activities. The canvasser is the most immediate channel of communication available between the party organisation and the electorate. When thinking in broad, national terms, one is inclined to assume that, so far as the major parties are concerned, such lines are equally available to all sections of the community. The Greenwich evidence indicates that this is not so. In the first place agents are reluctant to waste the energies of their workers in the strongholds of their enemy. Thus, when Transport House received a complaint that one of the Greenwich wards was not being adequately covered, and telephoned the Labour agent to that effect, our observer reported that the agent 'was a little vexed, but replied that he had no intention of covering it, since it was a strong Tory area'. Similarly, an observer present at a conference at Conservative headquarters late in the campaign reported: 'It was then decided to concentrate mobile squads of canvassers in North Ward, leaving St. Nicholas and North-West Wards out as there were too few Conservatives there to repay—those Conservatives being staunch and reliable souls who would vote anyway.' And this tendency of the agents to avoid the areas of opposition is of course reinforced by the selective canvassing of the ward helpers. In effect, then, the most socially homogeneous areas of a constituency such as Greenwich are scarcely 'contested', and residents in such areas have personal contact with only a single party. This external restriction of the 'conversation between the classes' (to use Professor Riesman's phrase) we shall find to be reinforced by subjective restrictions later in this study. It is important not to exaggerate the extent of these restrictions, and unfortunately we are in no position to offer a precise estimate. But from some 50 or 60 separate reports on canvassing expeditions and committee-room activities over the three weeks of campaigning the picture that emerges is fairly clear: it would seem that areas containing about 30% of the Greenwich population were canvassed by one party only, and that of the remaining areas, the 'middle wards' alone—containing some 40% of the population and most heterogeneous in their social composition—were canvassed with equal diligence by both.

Nomination day, February 13th, marked the mid-point of the campaign. In days when local journals had ample newsprint it was a day of some importance—photographs would appear of the candidates shaking hands as they handed in their papers, and the names of the more substantial assenters would be published. To-day the occasion has lost most of its local publicity value, and in Greenwich it passed off without ceremony or flash-bulbs. By mutual agreement each set of papers was signed by thirty assenters only. The Labour agent seems to have been alone in concerning himself about the social standing of his assenters—he spoilt his first set of papers by getting a peer of the realm to sign them, remembering too late that his Lordship did not enjoy the franchise. All candidates took care to get the signature of a substantial number of women: Mr. Gilbey, with ten female assenters, had the lowest number; Mr. Reeves, with fourteen, the highest.

After nomination day, the despatching of election addresses.

All candidates used for this purpose the one free postal delivery which the law allowed them; but there were marked differences in the way it was used. The Labour candidate's address was a large folded sheet, coming near in weight to the 2 oz limit. It had been designed to serve as a display poster as well (recipients were invited to place it in their windows), and the 55,000 copies printed cost £166. The candidate's name and photograph occupied the front page; inside was a summary of Labour policy and achievements, couched in heavily ethical terms—'If returned to Parliament for a second term, I will strive to defend the oppressed, to denounce injustice, to give service to those most in need of it'— while the back page invited readers to *work* as well as *vote* for the Labour cause, and listed nineteen addresses where help would be gladly accepted. In the course of four pages it found occasion to repeat the name 'Reeves' seven times.

Into the same envelope with this 'address' went a thin slip of paper intended to perform the same function as the 'poll cards' hitherto issued by the parties but now forbidden by law. The slip gave advice about polling procedure, and of course suggested (twice) that the vote should be given to Mr. Reeves.

The Conservatives issued no separate slip for this purpose; substantially the same information was printed on the back of the election address. (This led to a slight delay in distribution; for the first draft of the address contained an unfortunate piece of misinformation about the 'official poll card', and a thousand or two copies were printed before the error was discovered.) As finally distributed, Mr. Gilbey's address was a small folded sheet, neat and distinctive, about half the size of the Labour address; 62,000 copies were printed for a cost of £80. The 'pledges' contained in the text of the address followed the party's manifesto in general, but introduced under the heading of 'Education' a conscious bid for the Catholic vote—'I firmly believe in the right of all parents to have their children educated according to their religious beliefs, and I do not consider that they should be penalised financially for exercising that right.' (Local Catholic organisations had sought to obtain pledges of financial assistance for their schools from all three· candidates: Mr. Gilbey was the only one to comply.) The back page of the address contained a list of committee rooms— but no invitation to help in them—and a warning to car-owners not to take strangers to the poll.

In the same envelope with this address went a printed letter from the candidate's wife, and a leaflet bearing a message from Mr. Churchill. The six printed pages repeated the name 'Gilbey' five times (compared with nine mentions of the Labour candidate's name in five printed pages).

The Liberal address, smallest and most cheaply produced of the three (15,000 copies for £9), was crowded with small print setting forth Liberal policy, and mentioned the candidate's name three times in all. In the same envelope went a copy of the nationally produced 'Election Special'—a large four-page broadsheet publicising the party's leaders and policies.

In view of the new importance given to 'absent voters' under the Representation of the People Act of 1948, it is of interest to know how the parties dealt with these in making use of the free postal delivery. Our sample findings for December suggest that about 3,000 electors, whose names were on the Greenwich register, had removed from the borough or were away on business. The Conservative agent sent election literature to some 800 people in this category, the Labour agent to about 300, and the Liberal agent to none. It was here that the pre-campaign canvass of the Conservatives, mainly in the wards with the heaviest removal rates, proved valuable.

Apart from the election addresses both major parties made house-to-house deliveries of other election literature. The Conservatives had printed 45,000 of a 'pre-election' address (cost: £50) giving a brief biographical summary of Mr. Gilbey's career to date, which were handed to all who attended his meetings, and were slipped with other leaflets through letter-boxes. The Labour agent had printed a pre-poll 'Message to Electors' (60,000 at £114) which was systematically delivered from door to door during the last days of the campaign. And both parties, of course, distributed both at meetings and by canvassers great quantities of 'national' pamphlets and leaflets. All in all, the itemised election expenses show that 619,000 separate items of election literature were distributed by all parties—an average of 10 items for each elector. Nearly two-thirds of these emanated from the Conservative agent; of every 20 items distributed, 13 were Conservative, 6 Labour and 1 Liberal. It is clear that the Conservatives relied much more on printed publicity than the Labour agent—perhaps because their workers were more willing to distribute leaflets than to canvass. But it is worth remark that the Labour literature put out, both local and national, was much more elaborately and expensively produced than that of its rival; hence the printing and stationery bills of both parties were almost exactly the same in size—£491 odd.

Of this vast output, only two leaflets produced by the Conservative agent were sufficiently remarkable to call for special mention.

We have already described the dispute in Conservative ranks about the use to be made of the local housing 'scandal', in which the chairman had resisted attempts to make personal attacks on his Labour colleagues on the Council. In spite of his opposition, the decision was taken halfway through the campaign to issue a special leaflet setting forth 'the facts' about local housing. There was another issue, too, which raised questions of propriety. In the early days of his Government Mr. Reeves had made sympathetic references to the Soviet Union. 'Russia feels—she cannot help but feel —that Great Britain is "ganging up" with America against her . . . Russia wants peace more than any other country in the globe', he had told the Commons. Could one infer from this that Mr. Reeves was favourable to Communism? The Conservative candidate and his agent decided that one could. Again contrary to the wishes of the party chairman, they drafted a leaflet giving quotations from some of Mr. Reeves's speeches and carrying the slogan—'Reeves and Crypto-Communism or Gilbey and Conservatism'.

There was some fear in the Conservative office that, should news of these two special leaflets reach the Labour agent before they were fully distributed, he might attempt to suppress them by means of an injunction. They were therefore prepared with the greatest secrecy, delivered to the various committee rooms late on a Friday afternoon, and circulated the same evening by excited bands of helpers—some coming from outside the constituency for the occasion. It was hoped by this elaborate timing to ensure that householders would have two days to read them before the Labour agent could bring a copy before a magistrate.

When the first of these leaflets ('Crypto-Communism'— 25,000 copies printed in red and blue: cost, £51 13s.) reached the Labour agent he showed only a mild interest in it. 'So they're showing some fight at last!' was his first comment. And on later reflection he thought it generous of his opponents to spend their funds on giving side publicity to his candidate (in none of the Labour speeches or leaflets were the opposing candidates ever referred to by name). The reactions of the Conservative chairman were much more decisive. One of his party's main committee rooms was on his business premises. The morning after the leaflet was distributed all the posters were taken down out of the chairman's windows, and the committee room was closed. Two days later it opened again—but not before some very strong words had passed between candidate and chairman.

We were able to attempt a rough estimate of the effects of the 'Crypto-Communist' leaflet. On the Saturday morning following its distribution we sent out interviewers to obtain a small quota sample of opinions about it, and 81 interviews were secured from residents of the streets where it was known to have been delivered. 42 remembered having *seen* the leaflet, but only 28 had read it. Among these were 15 men—43% of all men in the sample; and 13 women—28% of all women in the sample. Thus the leaflet appeared to have attracted men more than women. The comments of these 28 people ranged from strong approval to strong disapproval, according to their pre-established political views. Opinions and vote intentions are related in the table below:

Table 8

ATTITUDE OF LEAFLET READERS RELATED TO VOTE INTENTION

	Vote Intention			
Comments	*Conservative*	*Labour*	*Liberal*	*Undecided*
Approving	8	—	1	—
Neutral	3	6	—	3
Disapproving	1	4	—	2
Total comments	12	10	1	5
Total in Sample	(38)	(28)	(4)	(11)

The sample is, of course, very small, and is probably subject to wide errors. But such as it is it suggests that the leaflet may have been read by 8,000–10,000 people. Approval of the leaflet was largely among the already converted; disapproval was spread among friends, enemies and the undecided. In short it seems probable that the leaflet secured a wide audience, and aroused stronger feelings than a leaflet usually contrives to do; but there is no evidence that the feelings were such as to advance the Conservative cause locally.

The 'Housing' leaflet was a much more modest affair (20,000 copies distributed: cost £9 10s.); and only about half of them were distributed on a house-to-house basis—the remainder were handed to passers-by in the streets or to audiences on their way in to Labour meetings. We were unable in these circumstances to take a sample poll of opinions about the leaflet; but our impression was that it was distributed too late in the campaign to secure much attention. One of our observers, in an outlying Conservative committee room, recorded the following note on the evening of its distribution. 'Conversation drifted on to the building leaflet, of which particularly the revelations under point 2 (low rents to socialist councillors) called forth general comment. The old woman seemed to have a few doubts, saying, "I wish they wouldn't sling mud, though." Reply was, "S'facts, clear facts." '

These two leaflets supplied the major 'incidents' of the

campaign, and their most marked effect was in the further disrupting of relations within the Conservative organisation. Apart from this, the control of the agents over their supporters was so pronounced that little happened in the constituency that had not been planned. Two or three minor acts of hooliganism, perpetrated against the Conservatives, afforded them valuable publicity in the local press and embarrassed the Labour candidate. The canvas roof of a Conservative councillor's car was slashed as it stood parked outside the Town Hall, and a quantity of Labour literature pushed through the slit. (In reporting the matter to the press, the councillor changed the incident slightly, to read, 'The contents of a dustbin was emptied into the car.') The window of a Conservative committee room on a main road was daubed with the legend 'Vote Labour' in red paint. Mr. Bulbrook received a telephone call from an anonymous man, threatening him with violence as 'a traitor to the working class'.

One other incident of the campaign deserves mention. Two days before polling-day the Liberal agent received a large supply of posters from his printer, and with the help of two other enthusiasts worked through the whole night to paste them on every as yet unused fly-poster site in the constituency. As a result of this feverish devotion, 500 more posters advertising the Liberal candidate's name were on view.

Unfortunately the agent got his posters mixed. The following morning Greenwich electors found themselves, as they passed some of the borough's bomb-sites, urgently invited to vote for the Liberal candidate for East Woolwich.

The campaign we have described in this chapter cost the three political parties jointly a total of £1,913. According to our estimates, rather more than 600 Greenwich electors devoted some 15,000 man-hours of their leisure to its prosecution. And as a background to these local activities there was for three weeks a steady torrent of election news and views pouring into every home from newspaper, magazine and radio. What were the effects of it all?

Chapter Six

THE SOCIAL GEOGRAPHY OF
POLITICS

THE first sample surveys of political opinion, made in
the United States during the thirties, produced a
double change in the interests of students of elections.
The research workers among them had hitherto devoted
most of their fact-gathering energies to the opinions and
activities of politicians and political organisations rather
than to those of the voters. The choice was forced upon them
by the evidence available. The careers and speeches of the
politicians were well documented; conclusions about the
motives of the electors rested on fragile inferences. The usual
procedure was to start from the election results and try to
find explanations for them in the issues which had figured
most prominently in campaign speeches; direct evidence
about what the electors thought or felt was rare, fragmentary
and unrepresentative. The sample survey made possible for
the first time the gathering of information directly from a
sample of electors as representative as systematic sampling
techniques could make it, and so the first change was a considerable increase in the amount of research attention given
to the electorate.

But the sample survey can answer some questions much
more easily than others, and the second change in focus was
a change in the type of question about the electorate which
was asked. People are given the opportunity of voting only
in one of a narrowly limited number of ways. But the motives
for voting one way or another, and the arguments used to

justify political choice may be infinitely varied and infinitely complex. A few unambiguous questions can tell us how people intended to vote at any one time. No one knows how many questions we would need to ask in order to find a complete answer to the question of why they voted as they did. Ask a factual question, and you will usually receive a straightforward answer. Certainly it may not always be the true answer. Precautions against misunderstanding and evasion are needed, but these present a comparatively simple problem compared with the difficultes facing any inquiry into motives. Ask a question about motives and you will often be answered by an uneasy stare and uninformative comment: 'I've always done it', 'It seems the best thing to do', or just 'I don't know.' Because a great many facts in past experience have contributed to any one human action, because often people have not reflected on their reasons for behaving as they do, and may be unaware of them, and because skill in self-expression is rare, to give even a schematic and superficial account of motives which will survive the most elementary tests of logic and reliability is a much more difficult task than to find out facts about people's behaviour or even intentions. It requires more extensive preliminary analysis of the problem to be studied,[1] more careful testing of the questions to be used (and there will usually be more of them), and more skill and patience in interviewing. For such reasons the 'pollsters', academic and commercial, have usually set about answering the question 'Who?' votes Conservative or Labour (or goes to the movies often, or takes a daily bath) with more confidence and in more detail than the question 'Why?'. A considerable body of knowledge about the interrelationships between facts of social position and political allegiances, about 'who' votes for this or that party, is gradually built up. This, incidentally, is an important preliminary to the study of 'why' people vote as they do, since detailed knowledge of the ways in which political choice varies among people with different social experience suggests many hypotheses about the reasons for choice.

[1] See, e.g., P. F. Lazarsfeld, 'The Art of Asking Why', *National Marketing Review*, Vol. 1, No. 1, Summer 1935.

So in turning from our description of political organisations in Greenwich to the relatively unorganised electorate,
we shall start by finding out how various groups voted. We
need make no apology for discussing first of all the differences
in political choice between rich and poor, the middle classes
and the working classes. Political observers have been point-
ing out for hundreds, if not thousands, of years that different
classes have different political ideas, and here the sample
survey has done no more than enable us to measure the differences somewhat more precisely. Nor will we spend time discussing how 'class' should be defined. One may define class
solely in terms of wealth, or by occupation, by the many
details of speech and taste and table manners that go to make
up a style of life, or by the degree of familiarity or deference
accorded to a person by his fellows. These and many other
attributes which tend to be introduced into discussion of the
meaning of class are fairly closely associated, so that a division
into broad classes based on any one of them would to a large
extent overlap with a division based on any other. Moreover,
whatever criterion is taken, any dividing line (and for statistical analysis a dividing line is a practical necessity) will be
arbitrary. In present-day Western society at least, social
classes shade imperceptibly into each other.

The best that we can hope to do is to choose a criterion
which is associated with class differences, even if it does not
include their whole meaning, and to bear in mind that the
precise magnitude of the statistical differences we find would
doubtless change were another index used. Our use of the
terms 'middle class' and 'working class' to describe the resulting groups can be regarded as a stylistic convenience.

Among the data gathered in the Greenwich survey there
are a number of indices of class position, two of which we
must now introduce. The first of these, whose general title
and differentiating labels are perhaps odd but have already
become hallowed by tradition, is 'Socio-Economic Status'.
The classification of our informants into socio-economic
grades is based on an assessment made on the spot by the
B.I.P.O. interviewers. At the close of each interview, the
informant was rated on a four-point scale. These ratings were

based chiefly on the average income level for the informant's occupation (or her husband's or father's), but were also influenced by such factors as apparent standard of living, accent, and general bearing. 'Average plus' was the highest grading, and represents a high level of economic prosperity. (3% of the sample were placed in this category.) 'D' was the lowest grading, and represents a level at or near the poverty-line. (The D grade includes 12% of our sample.) 'Average' and 'Average Minus' represent in general the economic levels associated with the mass of white collar workers and manual workers respectively. (18% of the sample were graded as 'Average' and 67% as 'Average Minus'.)

A second index is provided by the Hall-Jones status scale. This scale is a seven-fold classification of occupations in descending order of social prestige. The groups used were:

1. Professional and High Administrative.
2. Managerial and Executive.
3. Inspectional, Supervisory and other non-Manual, higher grade.
4. Inspectional, Supervisory and other non-Manual, lower grade.
5. Skilled Manual and routine grades of non-Manual.
6. Semi-skilled Manual.
7. Unskilled Manual.

Unlike many classifications of this kind which reflect only the judgment of their compilers, the Hall-Jones scale was tested by asking samples of the public to grade a list of occupations to make sure that the scale was 'not out of touch with the opinion of the man in the street'.[1] The test showed a very close conformity between the relative status accorded to each occupation by different groups of the public. In the Greenwich survey we asked the occupation of informants (or of the husbands of married women, and the fathers of single

[1] For a description of the procedure used, see John Hall and D. Caradog Jones, 'Social Grading of Occupations', *British Journal of Sociology*, Vol. 1, No. 1, March 1950, pp. 31–55.

women), and these were subsequently classified into the seven groups of the Hall-Jones scale.[1]

In the following discussion we will usually combine the categories of these indices to form two classes in each scale,[2] but differences in vote are first shown in Table 9, using the scales in a more extended form.

Table 9

CLASS DIFFERENCES IN VOTING

Social-Economic Status

	Av.+	Av.	Av.−	D
% of 1950 voters voting	%	%	%	%
Conservative	82	64	27	18
Labour	12	24	69	78
Liberal	6	12	4	4
N. (=100%)	(17)	(124)	(470)	(77)

Hall-Jones Scale

	1, 2 and 3	4	5	6 and 7
	%	%	%	%
Conservative	66	80	28	17
Labour	23	16	66	80
Liberal	11	4	6	3
N. (=100%)	(52)	(57)	(263)	(237)

As these two cross-tabulations show, the proportion who voted Conservative steadily decreased and the proportion who voted Labour steadily increased with each step down the social scale, whether we select income or occupational prestige as the chief criterion for placing informants. For example, to take the index which we shall use most often, the Socio-Economic Status Scale, among the 2% of our sample with the highest incomes, about 8 people out of 10 voted

[1] Unfortunately, for 14% of our sample we obtained insufficient information to enable us to classify the informant's occupation. For this practical reason we shall in most cases use the S.E.S. scale as our index of class position.

[2] We shall use the term 'middle class' to mean either Average+ and Average on the S.E.S. scale, or groups 1–4 on the Hall-Jones scale; and 'working class' to mean either Average− and D on the S.E.S. scale, or groups 5–7 on the Hall-Jones scale.

Conservative, and only about 1 in 10 voted Labour, while among the poorest 11%, less than 2 out of 10 voted Conservative, and nearly 8 out of 10 voted Labour. The two groups which were intermediate in wealth were more evenly divided in their vote, but again the better-off voted largely Conservative and less well-off largely Labour.

The pattern is in general similar if we take as our index the Hall-Jones scale, but in this case there is one irregularity in the progression from Conservatism to Labour as we descend the social hierarchy. People in Class 4 occupations (which were non-manual jobs requiring comparatively little skill and training and carrying no authority over others) voted Conservative even more often than those in the higher-prestige occupational groups. Because of the small numbers in the sub-groups the difference is not statistically significant, and it may well be due simply to 'sampling error'. It is, however, a difference worth watching for in future studies of the present kind. It may be that people in such occupations, on the fringe of the middle class, feel a need to safeguard their position by more strict conformity to middle-class norms where they have a choice, to make up for their inability, for financial reasons, to conform in other ways.[1]

The most interesting point about Table 9, however, is the wide gap in the proportions voting Conservative and Labour between the lower level of our 'middle class' ('Average' on the S.E.S. grading, and Grade 4 on the Hall-Jones Scale). and the upper level of the 'working class' ('Average Minus' on the S.E.S. grading, and Grade 5 on the Hall-Jones Scale).

[1] This speculation is given some plausibility by the fact that, when asked to name the social class to which they belonged, those in Grade 4 occupations were even more likely than those in the higher grades to call themselves middle class. The replies to this question for the four occupational groupings we have used are shown below.

OCCUPATION AND SELF-ASSIGNED CLASS

	1–3 %	*4* %	*5* %	*6–7* %
% saying they were				
Upper Middle Class	11	8	1	—
Middle Class	44	57	13	7
Lower Middle Class	21	15	12	5
Working Class	19	14	69	85
Don't know	5	6	5	3

This suggests that although finer class gradations might be distinguished by methods more subtle and exact than ours, we are justified both in speaking of two major classes, and in claiming that our indices give us an approximate and useful method of identifying their members. Because the differences in vote between socio-economic strata are so sharp (as we shall see, they are stronger than any other difference defined by objective attributes), and because class position is associated in greater or lesser degree with almost all other variables, we shall retain the division between middle class and working class in studying other group variations in vote.

Class position is only the most obvious of the ways in which voters for one party may differ from those of another. In any election-time discussion many more will be suggested—there will be references to a 'woman's vote' and a 'trade-union vote'; one party's platform will be said to appeal to the inexperienced voter, another to the educated man. In the following pages we will examine how far, within each social class, such further differences were associated with party choice.

Let us look first at the effect of age. Table 10 shows how people under 50 differed in their choice of party from those aged 50 and over, within each social class.

Table 10

AGE AND VOTE

S.E.S.

	Av.+ and Av.		*Av.— and D*	
Age	*21–49*	*50 and over*	*21–49*	*50 and over*
	%	%	%	%
% *voting*				
Conservative	63	67	18	42
Labour	24	23	79	53
Liberal	13	10	3	5
N. (=100%)	(93)	(49)	(359)	(186) ·

There appears to be some truth to the proverbial view that men are socialists in their youth and conservative in their old age. In each class, the young voted Labour more often and Conservative less often than the old. But this difference is only slight among the middle class; it is very strong among the working class. This suggests that the contrast is not simply due to the psychological changes produced by growing older. Perhaps it may stem from the historical differences in experience between the generations. The Labour Party is still a comparative newcomer to the political scene. A man of Mr. Churchill's age who had lived in Greenwich all his life would have reached middle age, and have voted in four General Elections, before he ever had a chance to vote for a Labour candidate.

While the younger members of the working class, when they voted for the first time, could already choose between the parties that stood for election in 1950, their elders had, in their youth, known only two of these parties. Many of them probably voted Conservative from the start (since it is unlikely that, before the advent of the Labour Party, the working class vote was as homogeneous as it is now) and, as we shall see in a later chapter, a political allegiance once established is not often changed. Others with an earlier allegiance to a party now defunct or declining, may have preferred to change to the familiar Conservative Party rather than to the new Labour Party, whose appeals were as novel as its name.

We shall next compare the vote decisions of men and women. The political commentator's analyses of the 'women's vote' imply that the two sexes make their decisions about how to vote on different grounds, and hence often support different parties. Table 11 provides the figures necessary to test this conclusion for our sample.

In both classes, women voted Conservative more frequently than men, although, as with age, the class differences greatly outweighed the sex differences. Why should this be so? Remembering that in England women tend to live longer than men, and that their average age is consequently higher, we may suspect that Table 9 merely repeats the findings of Table 8 in disguised form—that women were more Conservative because they were, on the average, older. Table 12, however, shows that age differences account for feminine Conservatism only in part.

Table 11

SEX AND VOTE

S.E.S. Sex	Av.+ and Av.		Av.− and D	
	M.	F.	M.	F.
	%	%	%	%
% voting				
Conservative	61	68	21	30
Labour	28	19	75	66
Liberal	11	13	4	4
Total (=100%)	(72)	(70)	(249)	(296)

Table 12

SEX, AGE AND VOTE

S.E.S. Age Sex	Av.+ and Av.				Av.− and D			
	21–49		50 and over		21–49		50 and over	
	M.	F.	M.	F.	M.	F.	M.	F.
	%	%	%	%	%	%	%	%
% voting								
Conservative	58	67	68	68	15	21	34	47
Labour	31	22	17	23	83	75	57	50
Liberal	11	11	15	9	2	4	9	3
N. (=100%)	(45)	(48)	(27)	(22)	(170)	(189)	(79)	(107)

The groups here become rather small, particularly in the middle class, for conclusions to be stated with complete confidence, but tentative inferences may be drawn. Women do, regardless of age, appear to be more conservative than men, but the magnitude of the difference varies in different class and age groups. In the middle class, it is strong only among the younger voters; among those over 50 it disappears. Among the working class, women of all ages are more conservative than men. The relationship between sex and vote is, however, not so marked as that between age and vote.

The older men, for example, vote Conservative more often than do the younger women.

That women are more conservative than men, not only in political affiliation and on specific political issues, but also in their views on a wide range of social customs, has become a commonplace among survey findings. Perhaps part of the explanation may be found by extending the reason suggested for an age difference in voting. If a Labour vote is a social novelty which the old, whose habits were fixed in an earlier period, adopt more reluctantly than the young, it may be that women lag behind because, in a changing world, their social contacts are more limited than those of men. From quite an early age, girls have to stay at home and help with the housework, while boys are out playing in the streets and parks. Men have to work for a living, and come in contact with other people in their jobs, but most married women stay at home. The informal sociability of the pub is much less open to women than to men. In short, many aspects of the outside world, including politics, often reach women indirectly, through the male members of their families, who act as intermediaries. This view is supported by the figures in Table 13 showing the replies to our question 'In the past three or four weeks, have you talked politics with anyone?'

Table 13

DIFFERENCES IN POLITICAL DISCUSSION BETWEEN MEN AND WOMEN

	Men	Women
% who talked politics with	%	%
Family	30	38
Friends	30	16
People at work	54	12
Others	18	14
No one, can't recall	27	51
N. (=100%)	(352)	(420)

Women talk politics less often than men, and when they do, it is mainly with their families. The most usual partners in male political discussion were workmates, and they reported talking with friends as often as with family members. We do not, of course, know which members of the family women talked with, but we need not conclude, from the difference in the proportions of men and women who reported family discussions, that a considerable fraction of them must have been other women. In the Sandusky Survey, the number of wives who reported political conversations with their husbands was very much larger than the number of husbands who reported talking to their wives, although in a randomly selected sample we would logically expect the numbers to be equal. The conclusion drawn was that the two sexes place unequal importance on these family discussions, and that 'men do not feel that they are discussing politics with their wives; they feel they are telling them.'[1]

It is possible then that women's political conservatism results partly from a greater social isolation which makes them slower than men to change their opinions and attitudes. While we cannot test this hypothesis completely with the data at our disposal, there is one inference to be drawn from it which we can test. If women to a great extent form their ideas on the pattern given by the members of their families, instead of sifting and selecting from a wider variety of social influences, we might expect that single women, more often following the lead of the older generation, in the person of their father, would be more conservative than married women with husbands of approximately their own age. The figures are shown in Table 14. Although, with the additional control of marital status, the numbers in each group become very small (it is only possible to present them at all for working class women), the differences are in the expected direction. In the working class, married women in each age group do vote Labour more often than single women.

Probably this comparative social isolation is only one factor among many at work in producing greater conservatism among women than among men. Differences in values and social aspirations doubtless contribute. The contrasts in social experience (and hence in knowledge) between men

---

1 Paul F. Lazarsfeld, Bernard Brelson and Hazel Gaudet, *The People's Choice*, New York, Columbia University Press, 1948, p. 141.

and women are more varied and complex than these passing speculations indicate. But we cannot pursue the problem further with data available to us.

Table 14

VOTING OF MARRIED AND SINGLE WORKING CLASS WOMEN

Age	21–49		50 and over	
	Married	Single	Married	Single
% voting	%	%	%	%
Conservative	20	29	46	54
Labour	76	68	51	46
Liberal	4	3	3	—
N. (=100%)	(158)	(31)	(73)	(37)

The variations in vote associated with other differences in social experience may be dealt with more briefly. We shall consider first education.

Table 15

S.E.S. EDUCATION AND VOTE

S.E.S. Last School Attended	Av.+ and Av.		Av.− and D	
	Higher*	Elementary	Higher	Elementary
	%	%	%	%
% voting				
Conservative	68	59	33	24
Labour	19	31	52	75
Liberal	13	10	15	1
N. (=100%)	(95)	(49)	(110)	(441)

* Under this heading we have included those who went to technical and business schools as well as those who went to secondary schools and universities.

Within each class, those with only elementary education are more likely to vote Labour and less likely to vote Conservative than are those with higher education. But the more educated usually obtain jobs which are better paid and carry more prestige than do those who never attended more than an elementary school, and it is possibly this fact, rather than any difference in intellectual training, which is reflected in Table 15. The introduction of education as a third variable probably does no more than provide us with a more refined socio-economic scale.

The association between religion and vote cannot be fully explored with our data because representatives of minority religions are too few to enable us to retain a class control, or to introduce new controls. But the fact that different religions appeal to different classes has been repeatedly emphasised ever since times when religion and politics were far more closely intertwined than they are to-day. Table 16 shows how each religious group in our sample voted.

Table 16

RELIGION AND VOTE

	C. of E.	Non-Conf.	Religion R.C.	Other	None
	%	%	%	%	%
Conservative	36	44	27	25	22
Labour	59	44	70	55	70
Liberal	5	12	3	20	8
N. (=100%)	(548)	(39)	(59)	(20)	(67)

The table yields one minor surprise in that the traditional link between non-conformity and radical politics is not sustained by our small group of chapel-goers. For the rest, Catholics and professedly irreligious are considerably to the left of the Established churchmen.[1]

A factor which, we would expect, would show an even closer association with vote than some of those already discussed is trade union membership. Table 17 shows the

[1] The relationship between Catholicism and Labour does not appear to be due, in our sample, to the Catholics having lower socio-economic status. On each S.E.S. level, Catholics voted Labour more often than Protestants.

relationship between union membership and vote. Informants who were not working have been omitted.

Table 17

UNION MEMBERSHIP AND VOTE

S.E.S.	Av.+ and Av.		Av.— and D	
Union Membership ?	*No*	*Yes*	*No*	*Yes*
	%	%	%	%
% *voting*				
Conservative	74	39	33	17
Labour	13	49	62	80
Liberal	13	12	5	3
N. (=100%)	(67)	(33)	(151)	(203)

Within each class members of a trade union were considerably more likely to vote Labour than were non-members. Even those whose income placed them in the middle class but who were members of a trade union voted Labour more often than they voted Conservative—the only group within the middle class, among those which we have examined, of whom this is true. Among working-class union members a minority, less than 1 in 5, still voted Conservative—but this is a proportion very much smaller than the 38% of working-class unionists which the Conservative Party claimed for itself at one time during the 1950 election campaign.

Table 17 does not, of course, show in which direction any causal relationship between union membership and a Labour vote works (nor even that a direct causal relationship exists). For many people union membership is an inevitable corollary of following a particular occupation and a more detailed study than ours would be needed to trace the importance of union activities in forming their allegiances. We shall show in a later chapter that Conservatives were more likely to desert their party if they belonged to a trade union. But it seems probable that the relationship is to some extent a circular one—that if union members become less Conservative, Conservatives are also less likely to join unions. This process of self-selection is probably more common in the middle class. However, the class-vote relationship remains stronger than the union-vote relationship. Middle-class union members are less likely to vote Labour than are those who belong to the working class but are not union members.

In this chapter we have been examining some of the relationships between the way people vote and facts about their social status and group memberships. One common finding has stood out in all the tables so far presented—that of the factors we have studied the one most strongly associated with differences in vote is social class. The other differences which have been traced, between men and women, old and young, those with only elementary education and those with higher education, and between trade union members and non-members, provide only minor variations on this dominant theme. The discussion has, however, been confined to variations in the proportions among these groups who voted for one or other of the two major parties. Before continuing, we must say something about the Liberal voters.

Since only a small number of our informants (6% of the sample) voted Liberal, and since they included people of all types, significant differences in the probability of a Liberal vote between sub-groups are difficult to trace. The proportions are shown in the preceding tables, and they will simply be summarised here. Again, the variable which shows the strongest relationship is social class: 12% of middle-class voters (S.E.S. Av.+ and Av) and only 4% of working-class voters (S.E.S. Av.— and D) chose the Liberal Party. Within the middle class there were few differences between sub-groups. In the working class it was the older men (Table 12) and the better educated (Table 15) who most frequently voted Liberal.

Chapter Seven

POLITICAL CHOICE AND VIEWS ABOUT CLASS

I N the previous chapter we showed that, of a number of objective facts about people's social position which were studied, the one most closely associated with choice of party was position in the hierarchy of social class. We defined class by means of an index based primarily on income. This procedure has often been criticised by social theorists who have put forward other types of definition. It would be out of place to discuss these here, since we lack the data for classifying our informants in most of the alternative ways that have been suggested, and in many cases to have collected such data would in itself have required a very complex research design and greater resources than we had at our disposal for the entire survey. But we can use one other type of criterion of class position—the way in which our informants themselves described their social class.

During the December interview members of the panel were asked: 'If you *had* to say which social class you belonged to, which would it be: upper middle, middle, lower middle or working?', a question which was answered by all but 5% of the sample. The majority of people assigned themselves to the same class as that in which they were placed by the S.E.S. index.[1] But interest will centre on the votes of those whose ideas about their own class position conflicted with

[1] For a discussion of the relationships between self-assigned class, S.E.S. and the Hall-Jones scale see Mark Benney and Phyllis Geiss, 'Social Class and Politics in Greenwich', *British Journal of Sociology*, Vol. 1, No. 4, pp. 311–16.

Political Choice and Views About Class

their apparent objective status. Did they vote with the class to which they felt they belonged or with the class whose economic situation they shared? In Table 18, informants are divided both by S.E.S. and by self-assigned class, and the distribution of votes for each of the four resulting groups is shown. The results appear at first to differ strikingly from those given in the previous chapter. Subjective class membership appears to show a much stronger relationship with vote than does objective class position.

Table 18

SOCIO-ECONOMIC STATUS, SELF-ASSIGNED
CLASS, AND VOTE

S.E.S.	Av.+ and Av.		Av.− and D	
*Self-assigned class**	*Middle*	*Working*	*Middle*	*Working*
	%	%	%	%
% voting				
Conservative	75	38	60	17
Labour	14	52	32	80
Liberal	11	10	8	3
N. (=100%)	(101)	(29)	(112)	(417)

* The three middle-class categories have been combined into one.

Our informants' views about the class to which they belonged coincided, in 4 out of 5 of the cases included in Table 16, with our own classification based on interviewers' ratings. Between the two groups whose class position was, in this sense, unambiguous, the contrast in political choice is sharp. Each group contained a dissenting minority, but three-quarters of those who were middle class both in income and in their own judgment voted Conservative, and an even higher proportion of those who were working class in both senses voted Labour. The two groups whose subjective class position differed from their objective position (objective at least in the sense that they did not make the assessment themselves) divided politically in proportions which were between these two extremes, but the subjective assessment appears to be associated with party choice much more closely than the objective assessment. The group who thought of themselves

115

as middle class although economically they belonged to the
working class, included 2 Conservatives to every 1 Labour
voter, and was much nearer in political composition to the
'pure' middle class than to the 'pure' working class. The
corresponding proposition about those who are objectively
middle class and subjectively working class also appears,
from the figures in Table 18, to hold good. But the number
of cases is far too small for confidence and, as will appear from
the following paragraphs, there are other reasons for
doubting it.

Table 19

S.E.S., SELF-ASSIGNED CLASS AND
OCCUPATION

S.E.S. Self-assigned class	Av.+ and Av.		Av.— and D	
	Middle %	Working %	Middle %	Working %
Hall-Jones grade				
1–3	38	18	1	1
4	37	5	6	1
5	17	56	45	39
6	—	3	21	29
7	—	—	7	18
Not classifiable	8	18	20	12
N. (=100%)	(101)	(29)	(112)	(417)

The figures in Table 18 suggest, then, that the way in
which a person thinks of his position in the class structure
has a stronger influence on the way he votes than do the
economic interests bound up with his objective position.
This conclusion, although obviously over-simplified, would,
if justified, have such a wide interest that it is worth closer
investigation. One possibility is that the apparent result may
be due simply to the crudity of our objective index of class
position.[1] Perhaps in the minority of ambiguous cases our

[1] But this is not revealed by using the S.E.S. index in its detailed form. All
except 5 of the informants whose S.E.S. was working class and whose self-
assessment was middle class were rated as 'Average—', but the 5 who were
rated 'D' all voted Conservative.

informants made a more accurate assessment of their real situation than our interviewers, with much scantier information, could achieve. We can to some extent check this hypothesis by using our second objective index, the Hall-Jones scale. It will be confirmed if the occupations of those in the two ambiguous groups are more like the occupations of those with whom they identify themselves than of those with whom they were classed by the S.E.S. index. Table 19 shows the Hall-Jones grading of occupations for the four groups we have been discussing.

It does seem to be true that the difference in distribution of votes between those who thought of themselves as middle class and those who thought of themselves as working class within each of our S.E.S. groups is *in part* accounted for by the crudity of our index. The two ambiguously classified groups occupy a position intermediate between the two 'pure' groups in occupation as well as in vote. In particular, over half of the small group with an S.E.S. of Av. + or Av. who apparently down-graded themselves into the working class were in occupations generally regarded as working class. The other ambiguous group, those with an S.E.S. of Av. − or D who had upgraded themselves into the middle class, tended to be in occupations carrying higher prestige than those of the 'pure' working-class group. We would expect them, therefore, to include a higher proportion of Conservative voters. But in their case occupational differences[1] appear to be by no means the whole story. Few of this group (those with Av. − or D S.E.S. who described themselves as middle class) had occupations rated as middle class, and more than a quarter belonged in the two lowest occupational grades. But the largest group came from Grade 5— 'skilled manual and routine grades of non-manual occupations'. People whose occupations are included in this grade have generally been labelled 'working class' by those who have used the Hall-Jones scale; and the majority of those with Grade 5 occupations described themselves as members of the working class.[2] But the group is heterogeneous in what

---

1 At least in so far as they are revealed by the Hall-Jones scale.
2 See above, p. 104, and Table 20 below.

may be an important respect. The majority of its members are skilled manual workers, but it also includes a number of 'white collar' occupations, the chief of which are shop assistants and people with routine and non-responsible office jobs, occupations which many people would want to call 'lower middle class' rather than 'working class'. We shall examine, therefore, the relationship between subjective class assessment and vote in this borderline occupational group. Table 20 shows the distribution of votes among self-described middle class and working class separately for three occupational levels.

Table 20

OCCUPATION, SELF-ASSIGNED CLASS, AND VOTE

Hall-Jones Occupational Grade	1–4		5		6–7	
Self-assigned Class	Middle %	Working %	Middle %	Working %	Middle %	Working %
% voting						
Conservative	74	67	59	15	37	13
Labour	15	27	31	82	52	85
Liberal	11	6	10	3	11	2
N. (=100%)	(85)	(18)	(71)	(74)	(27)	(201)

Let us consider first the groups whose occupations are the simplest to label in class terms—those in Grades 1–4, which are entirely white-collar occupations, and those in Grades 6–7, which are entirely manual occupations. Few of the former call themselves members of the working class, and few of the latter call themselves members of the middle class, so that these groups become too small for any firm conclusion to be drawn, but it appears that, although influenced by their own views about their class position, a majority in each case vote like the rest of their occupational equals.[1] It is in occupational grade 5 that the individuals' own judgment about his

[1] Cf. F. M. Martin, 'Social Status and Electoral Choice in Two Constituencies', *British Journal of Sociology*, Vol. III, No. 3, pp. 234–6. Mr. Martin's findings were similar although his occupational index was somewhat different from ours.

class position shows the strongest association with vote. In this grade, a majority of those who call themselves middle class voted Conservative, and a majority of those who call themselves working class voted Labour.

It is not possible to pursue the inter-relations between occupation, subjective class-assignment and political allegiance further with the Greenwich data. It may be that with a different occupational classification the association between occupation and vote would be even more regular. Possibly most of those with Grade 5 occupations who call themselves middle class are in white-collar occupations, although low-grade ones. But it seems probable that, whatever objective index of class position was devised, the research workers' categories would not always agree with people's own view of their class position, and that relationships with political allegiance similar to those seen above would be found. It may be, as suggested by Martin,[1] that the families and circles of friends of such persons would more often include people of varying social status and correspondingly varying political attitudes. But the factors which in England influence people's own view of their class position have been little studied up till now. It may be, on the other hand, that party allegiance is one of the factors which determines the sense of belonging to a particular class. Voting Conservative may be a cause as well as an effect of thinking of oneself as middle class, and voting Labour may be a reason for thinking of oneself as working class.

Other studies provide some support for this conclusion. In an unpublished national opinion survey made in 1953 the question: 'What would you say are the main social classes in this country?' was asked, and some people replied with the names of political parties. Although these only amounted to 5% of the replies, they do suggest that the issues of class and politics are not always distinguished. The most detailed study yet made of public definitions of social classes is that of Centers,[2] made in the United States. When asked what

[1] *Op cit.*, p. 236.
[2] R. Centers, *The Psychology of Social Classes*, Princeton University Press, 1949.

things it was important to know in deciding whether a person
belonged to their own class or not, more than twice as many
of his informants mentioned 'beliefs and attitudes' as mentioned 'money'. Problems in this area are receiving a good
deal of research attention at present, and these interrelationships will probably be clarified in the future. Meanwhile it
is clear, both from the Greenwich findings, and from those of
other English election surveys, that subjective views of class
position are of most help as predictors of vote in the case of
people whose incomes and occupations are on the borderline
between middle class and working class.

The basic fact that there is a sharp class division in the
way people vote, however, remains unaltered by these
difficulties and obscurities. Whatever definition we use,
most members of the middle class are found to vote Conservative, and most members of the working class to vote
Labour. Political allegiances are in fact formed along class
lines. But how far is this pattern reflected in what people
think about the parties? Is the Conservative Party generally
thought to stand primarily for middle-class interests, and the
Labour Party for working-class interests?

In December we asked our informants: 'From what you
know, which of the parties would do the best job for the
upper class? How about the middle class? And the working
class?' Table 21 shows the replies which intending voters
for the two major parties made to these questions, analysed
separately according to informants' assessments of their own
class position.

A first conclusion to be drawn from this table is that the
question was, for most people, a meaningful one. Few were
unable to answer it, at least for one class, although a small
minority among Conservative voters do appear to reject the
whole question. Ideas about which party would best serve
the interests of the 'upper class' were equally clear—irrespective of party or class, the answer was the Conservative
Party.

There was no such unanimity between the four groups of
voters about how the concerns of the other two classes were
to be furthered. The answers suggested by actual vote

Table 21

VIEWS ON WHICH PARTY WOULD DO THE BEST JOB FOR EACH CLASS

Self-assigned Class Vote Intention	Middle		Working		All
	Conservative	Labour	Conservative	Labour	Informants*
	%	%	%	%	%
Best party for *Upper Class†*					
Conservative	82	93	74	74	73
Labour	2	2	3	11	6
Liberal	—	5	4	1	2
Don't know	14	—	19	14	18
Best party for *Middle Class†*					
Conservative	75	10	58	19	36
Labour	—	60	8	40	23
Liberal	8	19	10	12	13
Don't know	12	10	22	28	25
Best party for *Working Class†*					
Conservative	49	—	54	—	18
Labour	29	98	24	92	63
Liberal	3	—	8	—	4
Don't know	15	2	14	5	13
N. (=100%)	(160)	(42)	(104)	(356)	(842)

* In addition to informants in the four groups analysed in the table, this column includes the replies of those whose vote intention was Liberal or undecided.

† Percentages do not always add to 100 because a few informants named parties not listed.

alignments, that the Conservative Party would do the best job for the middle class and the Labour Party for the working class, were by no means always accepted. These beliefs do appear as a trend underlying the answers, strengthening some groups in their beliefs and weakening others, but they were outweighed by two other tendencies. Firstly a majority of each group felt that the party it intended to vote for would do the best job for its own class. Middle-class Conservatives believed that the Conservative Party would do the best job for the middle class, working-class Labour voters that the Labour Party was best for the working class; but middle-class Labour voters thought the Labour Party best for the middle class, and working-class Conservatives thought the Conservative Party best for the working class.

The second tendency is the belief that one's own party will also do the best job for the *other* class. This answer, implying that there is no fundamental conflict of interests between classes, is the one most frequently given by each group, although it was not quite so popular as the belief that one's own party would do the best job for one's own class. Three-quarters of the middle-class Conservatives chose the Conservative Party for their own class, half of them chose it for the working class also. Nine out of 10 working-class Labour voters chose the Labour Party for their own class, 4 out of 10 chose it for the middle class also. Thus the most common pattern of belief was one that implies a harmony of interest between the classes.

In all, 80% of informants with a definite vote intention thought that the party for which they were going to vote would do the best job for their own class. Opinions about the welfare of the other class were more varied. Only a minority (although by no means an insignificant one—19% of the total) seemed to believe that the interests of the other class were so firmly opposed to their own that they would be better fostered by the rival party. Others avoided these implications of civil strife by saying that they did not know which party was best for the other class, or by naming the least dangerous of the contestants, the Liberal Party. But the pattern of answers given by the largest number was that the party of their choice would best serve *both* classes (49% in all gave this reply).

Although the replies were thus shaped by party loyalty and by some notion of the general good, the Labour Party was more often identified with the interests of the working class than the Conservative Party with those of the middle class. This is suggested by the total distribution of answers to the two questions, shown in Table 19. In all, the Labour Party was named as best for the working class almost twice as often as the Conservative Party for the middle class. This result is strongly coloured by the fact that a majority of our informants were Labour voters. But a similar difference appears when vote intention is held constant. The Labour Party's claim to represent the working class was whole-heartedly accepted by Labour voters and conceded by a fairly large group of Conservative voters (including, curiously, about a quarter of those who felt that they themselves belonged to the working class). Conservative voters, even when they thought of themselves as middle class, were less sure that the Conservative Party would further middle-class interests, and Labour voters seldom admitted it. We cannot, however, conclude that the Labour Party was more strongly identified with sectional interests than the Conservative Party, since the largest bloc of answers to these questions were those which committed the welfare of the 'upper class' to the Conservatives. Unfortunately we do not know who composed the upper class in the minds of our informants, but, whoever they were, it appears that any widespread feeling of class antagonism was confined to them. Labour voters who thought that the Conservative Party would do the best job for the upper class provide the only case in which a majority of voters thought that a party other than their own would best serve any class.

The questions discussed above were not framed in terms of reasons for choice, and it is conceivable that while each person believes that his own party will do the best job for his own class, this belief may be of minor importance for his decision to support that party. We did, however, ask informants to give us the main reason for their vote intention. The answers were so varied that few conclusions can be drawn from them, but the largest single group was references to class and group interests, made by 26% of informants. These were given largely by people who intended to vote Labour —42% of them replied by some direct reference to class interests, as compared with 5% of people who intended to vote Conservative. Among Conservatives no one group of answers predominated, although they were more likely than Labour supporters to reply in terms of economic policies, of abstract conceptions such as freedom, and of administrative efficiency. While the difference between the two parties in the number who directly referred to sectional interests is large, it may also be misleading, since many of the Conservative replies couched in terms of policy may have been indirectly concerned with class interests.

Chapter Eight

THE PERSONAL INVESTMENT

W̱E have now examined in some detail the way in which the people of Greenwich distributed their political preferences. But politics mean more than just the marking of a ballot paper. We have not yet gained any idea of their importance in the lives of our informants, nor of what they knew and thought about, and expected from, the parties for which they were voting.

For a start, although most of our informants voted, they are unlikely to have weighed the consequences of their vote with equal care and in the light of equal knowledge about the events of recent years; unlikely to have been equally absorbed by the news from Westminster in their daily papers. Our sample may have included people with all degrees of interest in politics, from the habitual non-voter who rarely read a newspaper and could scarcely manage to tell you who Mr. Churchill is, to the enthusiast who gave up all his spare time to politics and talked of little else. We asked our informants in December how much interest they had in politics, and gave them a choice of three answers: 'very, moderately, or not very interested'. Although we might have expected many people to avoid the third alternative as self-condemnatory, almost half our sample admitted that they were 'not very interested' in politics. A little over a third described themselves as 'moderately interested', and about 1 in 10 as 'very interested'. In most of the following tables we have combined these replies into two groups; the 'interested' ('very' and 'moderately') and the 'uninterested' (including the 6% who did not know how to describe themselves).

We are concerned to find out how interest in politics varied within the community, not only because of its importance for an understanding of reactions to the campaign, but for another reason. The findings of most of the election surveys made in recent years have indicated that the most important factor in getting people to the polling booths and in determining how they vote, is probably personal influence—the persuasion of their families, friends and acquaintances. The evidence for this hypothesis to be found in the Greenwich data will be discussed in a later chapter. The question of who these influential associates are has so far received comparatively little study. But, whatever other characteristics these associates may have, it seems probable that they are usually people with a more-than-average interest in politics. If this is so, it is doubly important to find out who the interested are. In Table 22, therefore, we show how interest varied among people with different social characteristics.

Middle-class people (whether so called by themselves or by the B.I.P.O. interviewers) were considerably more likely to describe themselves as interested in politics than were those in the working class; and men were much more interested than women. Age makes little difference—interested persons were equally common in each age group. Trade union membership appears to do a great deal to stimulate interest, for although members are largely working class they were much more often interested than were non-members.

Two of the strongest differences in levels of interest are those associated with class position and with sex. In Table 23 we give a more complex breakdown, so that the effect of these two characteristics can be compared.

We can see from Table 23 that interest in politics varies independently with both socio-economic position and sex. However, some of the differences in interest between the four groups of middle-class and working-class men and women are small. Working-class men are only slightly less interested than middle-class men. But working-class women are very much less interested than any other group. Less than

Table 22

INTEREST IN POLITICS AND SOCIAL CHARACTERISTICS

	Interested %	Uninterested %	N. (=100%)
Socio-economic status			
Av.+ and Av.	71	29	(172)
Av.—	46	54	(560)
D	34	66	(100)
Self-assigned class			
Middle	61	39	(251)
Working	44	56	(533)
Age			
21–39	49	51	(185)
30–49	49	51	(342)
50–64	53	47	(187)
65 and over	47	53	(118)
Sex			
Men	64	36	(377)
Women	38	62	(456)
*Union Membership**			
Member	61	39	(259)
Non-Member	52	48	(246)
Education			
Elementary	44	56	(608)
Higher	65	35	(225)

* Those not working have been excluded.

Table 23

INTEREST IN POLITICS AMONG MIDDLE-CLASS AND WORKING-CLASS MEN AND WOMEN

The figures show the percentage in each group who said they were either very or moderately interested in politics. Numbers in parentheses indicate the bases for the percentages.

S.E.S.	Men	Women
Av.+ and Av.	75% (80)	67% (80)
Av.— and D	63% (271)	31% (340)

a third of them are interested, compared to about two-thirds or more in each of the other groups. In this respect, at least, the sex difference in culture patterns is very much wider in the working class than in the middle class. In the middle class, the world of politics is open to all. In the working class it is largely a man's world.

Our method of classification into 'interested' and 'uninterested' may seem an over-simple one, and it may be doubted whether such phrases as 'not very interested in politics' are used in the same way by members of these different groups. People probably assess their own degree of interest by comparing themselves with their acquaintances and friends. We would expect, for example, a person who spent five minutes every morning reading the political news in his daily paper, but whose acquaintances often spent several hours studying all the papers, to call himself 'not very interested', while another person, who also spent five minutes on the political news but whose friends rarely did more than read the headlines over someone's shoulder in the bus, might describe himself as 'very interested'. In psychological terminology, we would expect judgments about interest in politics to depend on the frame of reference, and that in turn to vary with social status and role, and with group memberships.

We can to some extent test how far a process of this kind has affected these self-judgments of interest by using another criterion of interest—political knowledge on a very simple level. We know how many of our informants could, at the time of our first interview, tell us the party and name of their local Member of Parliament. How much variation is there between people who described themselves as 'interested' at different social levels in their ability to recall these names, and how much difference is there between men and women? The answers are shown in Table 24.

Ability to recall the party and name of their M.P. does vary with social position, even when the self-judged degrees of 'interest' are held constant, in the ways our hypothesis would lead us to expect. Interested middle-class people were better informed than interested working-class people, and interested men than interested women. However, these differences were smaller than those between the interested and the confessedly uninterested within the same class or sex. The phrases we used in our question do mean somewhat different things to different people, but, other things being equal, the 'interested' were much better informed than the 'uninterested'. The variations between classes and between men and women are not so great as to make the question useless as a basis of classification.

Table 24

INTEREST AND KNOWING PARTY AND NAME OF M.P.

	Percentage who knew		
	Party of M.P. %	Name of M.P. %	N. (=100%)
S.E.S.			
Interested			
Av.+ and Av.	82	39	(122)
Av.− and D	77	36	(290)
Uninterested			
Av.+ and Av.	54	22	(50)
Av.− and D	51	19	(370)
Sex			
Interested			
Men	84	41	(240)
Women	72	30	(172)
Uninterested			
Men	69	24	(137)
Women	42	20	(284)
Total	64	26	(833)

Table 24 provides another indication—which speaks for itself—of the general level of political interest in the constituency in the fact that, in all, only about 6 people out of 10 could name even the party of their local Member of Parliament. It is largely the uninterested women who account for this low average. On the other hand few in any group knew the name of their M.P.: among the best informed, the interested men, 4 out of 10, and for the sample as a whole only 1 in 4.

As we have seen, there were comparatively high proportions of people interested in politics in the middle class, among men rather than women, and among trade union members. We have suggested that these interested people are likely to have a comparatively strong influence over the way in which their associates vote. But we would expect this to happen only if the politically interested themselves have firm and decided political loyalties. All our evidence suggests, however, that they are more definite in their allegiances and more firmly committed to their party than are the uninterested. The answers to three of the questions which support this view are shown in Table 25.

Table 25

POLITICAL COMMITMENT AMONG THE
INTERESTED AND THE UNINTERESTED

	Interested %	Uninterested %
First vote intention		
Conservative	38	30
Labour	51	53
Liberal	4	3
Don't know	7	14
*Likely to change your mind**		
No	84	76
Perhaps, don't know	16	24
Party supporter†		
Yes	58	21
No	42	79
N. (=100%)		

The questions were:
  * 'Do you think you might perhaps change your mind before the election?' (This was asked after the question on vote intention.)
  † 'In general, would you call yourself a supporter of any political party?'

The Personal Investment

The interested appear to hold firmer convictions than the uninterested. They show less indecision about how they will vote, consider that they are less likely to change their minds and are more likely to call themselves party supporters. These questions, however, represent our informants' own description of themselves eight weeks before the election. A severer test of this party loyalty is given by their eventual behaviour on polling day. Table 26 relates February vote to December vote intention among the interested and the uninterested.

Table 26

CHANGES IN PARTY ALLEGIANCE AMONG
THE INTERESTED AND THE UNINTERESTED

Vote Intention	Interested		Uninterested	
	Conservative %	Labour %	Conservative %	Labour %
1950 Vote				
Conservative	90	1	73	5
Labour	4	91	12	85
Liberal	3	4	6	1
Did not vote	3	4	9	9
N. (=100%)	(134)	(197)	(108)	(196)

Those who were interested in politics seldom changed their minds about how they would vote. The changers were, for the most part, people who confessed that they had 'little or no' interest in politics. Similarly, non-voting was more than twice as frequent among the uninterested as among the interested.

Of the figures on the relationship between interest and party loyalty presented above, the strongest support for the hypothesis that it is among the politically interested that the 'unofficial party workers' are to be found is probably given by those on 'party support'. Almost 6 out of 10 among the interested described themselves as party supporters; only about 2 out of 10 among the uninterested did so. 'Party support' is a vague phrase which gives little information

131

about what these people in fact did to help their party, but a follow-up question asked for information on this subject. The answers are shown in Table 27.

Table 27

WAYS IN WHICH SUPPORTERS HELPED THEIR PARTY

	Vote intention of supporters	
	Conservative	Labour
	%	%
Hold office at present	2	*
Speaking, canvassing, other help in past month	3	5
Attended party meetings in past month	12	15
Defended party viewpoint in discussions in past month	35	42
Enrolled as member	41	28
None of these things	36	45
N. (=100%)	(129)	(183)

Percentages add to more than 100, as some supporters named more than one activity.

* Less than 1%.

Apparently quite a large number of people were prepared to call themselves party supporters although they gave their party little more than their goodwill and their vote. Over a third of Conservative supporters and almost half the Labour supporters could not specify any recent effort on behalf of their party. However, the Conservatives were not as well served by their supporters as this difference seems to suggest, for formal but passive membership of the party organisation was more common among them than among Labour supporters. Labour supporters were somewhat more likely to have given help by speaking or canvassing, to have attended party meetings, and (the type of active assistance most commonly reported) to have defended their party viewpoint in discussion. In all, about 1 in 5 of our sample claimed to have helped one of the parties in some way.

39% of the 'party supporters' (or 14% of the sample)

The Personal Investment

claimed to have helped their party during the month preceding our interview by defending its viewpoint in discussion. We have no record of where and with whom these
discussions took place, but some indication is given by the
answers to a question on 'talking politics'. Table 28 lists the
people with whom supporters and those who would not call
themselves supporters of a party, although they gave a definite vote intention (for convenience, they will be called
'followers'), had talked politics during the three or four weeks
before the first interview.

Table 28

POLITICAL DISCUSSION AMONG PARTY
SUPPORTERS AND FOLLOWERS

	Vote Intention			
	Conservative		Labour	
	Supporter	Follower	Supporter	Follower
	%	%	%	%
Talked with				
Family members	57	38	40	26
Friends	38	26	31	9
People at work	33	20	55	22
Publicans, shopkeepers,				
canvassers	20	7	13	5
Strangers	15	8	9	5
No one, don't recall	22	44	24	55
N. (=100%)	(129)	(146)	(181)	(234)

Percentages add to more than 100 because some informants
reported several conversations.

Evidently not all these discussions were controversial,
since the number of party supporters who had talked politics
was larger than the number who had 'defended their party
viewpoint in discussion'. Party supporters recalled more
conversations than did 'followers'. The most frequent type
of discussion was within the family circle, for all groups
except 'supporters' of the Labour Party, who talked politics
more at work than at home. Discussion at work was in

general more important for Labour voters than for Conservatives, while the latter talked more with friends.

Party supporters were not only more likely to have talked
politics than were followers, but they were more likely to
have participated in each separate type of discussion—at
work, with friends, with the family, etc. This last difference
—that party supporters discuss politics more within the
family than do followers—suggests that party support tends
to be a family affair, so that if one member supports one of
the parties, other members of the family do also.[1]

Although we started this chapter by discussing interest in
politics, the above tables have been based on the division
between party supporters and followers instead of on that
between interested and uninterested. The two classifications
overlap to a considerable extent. Of the self-described party
supporters, 73% said they were interested in politics, and of
the followers only 34%. 'Party supporters' were drawn from
the same social groups as were the 'interested in politics'.
They were more often found among men, in the middle class
(although the difference between the classes was not as great
as in the case of 'Interest'), and among trade union members.
There was only one difference in the incidence of answers
to the two questions. Older people were no more likely to
say that they were interested in politics than were the young,
but they *were* more likely to describe themselves as party
supporters. (The answers of different age groups to the question on party support are shown in Table 29.) The idea of
party support apparently includes that of continued support
over a period of time.

In spite of apparent differences in meaning between the
two questions we have been discussing, they can in practice
serve as roughly interchangeable indices for separating out
the people who are most likely to influence the views of their
fellows. However, because the question on talking politics is
of central importance when considering these interpersonal
influences, Table 30 gives the answers again, controlled by

[1] This hypothesis could only be confirmed by more direct information. The
difficulty of drawing indirect inferences from this type of question has been
indicated above, p. 109.

The Personal Investment

degree of interest in politics and by socio-economic status. (The latter control overlaps very considerably with that used in the earlier table, vote intention.) The differences which appear in this table are in general similar to those in Table 28, but some points are revealed more clearly.

Table 29

AGE AND PARTY SUPPORT

	Age Group			
	21–29 %	30–49 %	50–64 %	65+ %
Supporters	36	39	42	45
Followers	64	61	58	55
N. (=100%)	(186)	(345)	(183)	(118)

Table 30

POLITICAL DISCUSSION AMONG INTERESTED AND UNINTERESTED PERSONS IN EACH SOCIAL CLASS

S.E.S.	Av.+ and Av.		Av.− and D	
Interest in politics	Interested %	Uninterested %	Interested %	Uninterested %
Talked with				
Family members	52	41	43	24
Friends	48	22	31	7
People at work	39	26	51	13
Publicans, shop-				
keepers, canvassers	20	7	13	5
Strangers	15	8	9	5
No one, can't recall	22	44	24	55
N. (=100%)	(122)	(50)	(290)	(370)

The interested had discussed politics considerably more than had the uninterested, a difference which is particularly marked in the working class. Among all groups except the politically interested working class the most common type of discussion was that among members of the family. Like party supporters as compared to followers, the interested reported each type of conversation more frequently than did the uninterested. But although the interested talked politics at home more often, family discussions formed a smaller proportion of the total for them than for the uninterested. Among the interested, the proportions of discussions reported which were with family members were 29% in the middle class and 30% in the working class. Among the uninterested they were 43% and 48% respectively.[1] The politically interested probably had more influence than the uninterested within the home, but they were also more active in spreading their views outside the home—at work, with friends, and in a variety of other social situations.

Table 30 has provided some confirmation of the hypothesis that the politically interested were likely to have the most influence over whether or not other people voted, and over the way they voted. And, from what we know of the characteristics of the interested, men are likely to have been more influential than women, and trade union members than non-members. Because of social and psychological restrictions on 'the conversation between the classes', it is doubtful whether a similar conclusion can be made about the middle class as compared with the working class. Perhaps the correct inference is that the barrage of persuasive talk is heavier in the middle class than in the working class.

Political discussion is not merely a means for influencing others (either consciously or unconsciously), but also of acquiring political knowledge. We asked informants where they got their information about politics from, and showed them a list of sources. Table 31 compares the replies of the interested and the uninterested.

The interested drew their information from very varied sources. For them, as for the uninterested, the daily newspaper was the most important source of news, but politics are more intimately linked with social activity for them than for the uninterested. 'Talking to people' was the reply second in frequency of mention, and both this answer and

[1] Each of the answers listed in Table 30 might cover several discussions, and details about the number of discussions held might give different proportions.

136

'going to meetings' were given much more often by the interested than by the uninterested. On the other hand radio, the medium which demands least activity, has a relatively greater importance for the uninterested. Among them, it almost equals newspapers in frequency of mention, and it is the only medium which they named as often as did the interested. These differences between the two groups cut across class barriers. For those interested in politics, whether middle class or working class, contact with other people is the typical way of keeping informed. For the uninterested in both classes it is the radio.

Table 31

INTEREST IN POLITICS AND SOURCE OF
POLITICAL INFORMATION

	Interested %	Uninterested %
Sources mentioned		
Newspapers	81	63
Talking to people	65	29
Radio	61	61
Meetings	23	4
Newsreels	16	11
Magazines	15	5
Don't know	*	12
N. (=100%)	(412)	(421)

* Less than 1%.

The importance placed on talking to people as a source of information may seem odd in these days when radio and the daily press reach almost everyone. But talk has a warmth and life which the mass media, remote and impersonal, lack. It can, moreover, mediate between the individual and other sources, drawing his attention to facts and points of view which he may have missed. Although we did not explore in detail the uses our informants made of the information they got from personal discussion, we did ask them which source of information they thought most reliable. This time, few replied 'talking to people'. For both interested and uninterested, radio was regarded as the most reliable source (40% of the sample gave this answer), followed by newspapers (22%). 13% of the sample thought other people the most reliable source of news. This question showed little difference between interested and uninterested except that, as almost invariably, more of the uninterested had no definite opinion.

In this chapter we have compared those who claimed to have at least a moderate interest in politics with those who admitted to little or no interest. That these self-assessments of our informants were reasonably reliable is suggested by the facts that the interested were better informed and had more definite opinions, that they joined in political discussion more often, and that they drew on a wider variety of sources for their political information than did the uninterested. Political interest was more common in the higher than in the lower socio-economic grades, and among men than among women. Two further differences between interested and uninterested emerged. Politics is for the interested more a part of social activity among their fellow men and less simply a spectacle to be absorbed through the mass media of communication; and they are more firmly committed to the party for which they have decided to vote. Other characteristics of the politically interested will be described in later chapters.

Chapter Nine

VOTE INTENTION AND OPINIONS
ON PARTY POLICY

I N the last chapter, differences in the degree of interest
in politics which our informants felt, and in their judgments of themselves as supporters of a party were
examined, as part of the background to study of their
behaviour during the election campaign. But if the members
of our panel did not meet the campaign with equal interest,
neither did they meet it with equally open minds about the
issues over which the election was fought. In the present
chapter, opinions on party policies and party capabilities,
on the chances of victory, and on what was expected to
happen after the election will be described.

During 1949, each of the major parties had prepared for
the coming election by issuing a statement of policy. The
Labour Party document, 'Labour Believes in Britain', and
its Conservative reply, 'The Right Road for Britain', were
not, either in their language or their ideas, sharply opposed
documents. They showed clear traces of an unwillingness to
offend any section of the electorate; and it was not easy to
unravel, from among their many polite professions, any set
of clear, unambiguous principles which embodied the main
differences between the two parties. Yet to arrive at any
estimate of the relations between policy and votes it was
necessary to get our informants' views on a number of issues
arising from party disputes. We settled finally on ten controversial statements, five from each of the two chief policy
statements. To ensure that their partisan character was

recognisable, we pre-tested our selections both with party officers and with relatively informed members of the public, and they were unfailingly attributed to the right sources. We feel confident, then, that at the time of our first interview the following propositions reflected major points of disagreement between the two main parties:

Conservative Propositions

1. State trading leads to high prices.
2. Controls should be taken off private builders.
3. Socialism is a stepping-stone to Communism.
4. The union 'closed shop' is wrong in principle.
5. Our foreign policy should be based on 'Empire First'.

Labour Propositions

6. The workers should have more control in industry.
7. Government planning is essential for full employment.
8. Large inequalities of wealth and privilege are wrong.
9. All basic industries should be nationalised.
10. Native people in our Empire should have self-government soon.

These propositions, in which the language of the party pamphlets has been retained as far as possible, were presented to informants in random order, with a brief neutral explanation of the terms used where this seemed desirable. They were introduced with the remark: 'Here are a number of things that people say. Do you think that they are true, or untrue?'

A considerable number of informants (the average for all items was 20%) had no opinion at all about these issues, although the number of 'don't knows' naturally varied from one item to another. The greatest crystallisation of opinion was on the two issues of building controls and nationalisation. (The first of these was treated by both parties as one of the major election issues, and the second, although rather played down by the Labour Party, had been in the forefront of public discussion since 1945.) Only 14% had no opinion on

Vote Intention and Opinions on Party Policy

these two issues. On the other hand, the proportion who had no opinion was above average for two other issues—native self-government (30% did not know what they thought), and state trading (26%). The first of these was not a dominant issue in the election, and, as will be seen, opinions about it were not sharply divided on party lines. The above average proportion with no opinion on the question of state trading may have been due to genuine indecision, but it seems more probable that a comparatively high proportion of people did not understand what our statement was about.

We have discussed first the degree to which our informants had any definite opinion on these issues in order to simplify the presentation of what their opinions were. Table 32 shows the proportions who agreed with each of the items, among those who intended to vote for each of the major parties.

Table 32

VIEWS ON PARTY POLICY STATEMENTS*

Policy item	% agreeing with each item among whose vote intention was	
Conservative	Conservative	Labour
Building controls	81	45
State trading	78	31
Closed shop	69	43
Socialism	68	21
Empire first	78	65
Labour		
Full employment	46	79
Workers' control	31	63
Equality	37	58
Nationalisation	7	49
Native self-government	36	54
N. (=100%)	(277)	(420)

* Conservative statements have been arranged in the order of support given to them by Conservatives, and Labour statements in the order in which they were supported by Labour adherents, except that the two items on Imperial questions have been placed at the bottom of their respective lists.

It is difficult to decide which is the more remarkable feature of this table, the extent of agreement, or the extent of disagreement between the parties. For each item there was a large difference between the parties, in the proportion of those expressing agreement. More Conservatives agreed with each of their own party's propositions than agreed with any of the Labour propositions, and similarly, with one exception, Labour adherents supported all the Labour items more strongly than any of the Conservative items. (The exception, the Conservative statement that foreign policy should be based on 'Empire First', was accepted as true by Labour supporters more often than any Labour statements except that on full employment.)

On the other hand, substantial minorities agreed with each of the opposing party's propositions, with the exception of that on nationalisation (which was rejected almost unanimously by Conservatives). Moreover, within the limit placed by the tendency to agree most fully with one's own party, propositions which received strong support from one party tended to receive comparatively strong support from the other also. For example, the attack on building controls was the most popular Conservative plank, both among Conservatives and (next to the Empire First proposition) with Socialists; just as the statement on full employment and government planning received more agreement from both than any other Labour proposition; for both parties nationalisation was the least popular of the Labour proposals, and the slogan 'Socialism is the stepping-stone to Communism' the least popular of the Conservative proposals. This overlapping of opinion is of considerable importance. It indicates the degree to which we are justified in speaking of 'public opinion' rather than of a number of distinct 'group opinions'. The extent of common opinion, even on 'controversial' issues, between those who support different political parties certainly contributes a great deal to making the smooth working of democratic processes possible.

This overlapping of opinion, or tendency to agree with both parties, becomes even more striking if the percentages of those agreeing are based on the numbers who had a positive _opinion, excluding those who did not know what they thought. These figures are given in Table 33. They show that two Labour propositions (those on full employment and on native self-government) were accepted by Conservative voters more often than they were rejected; and that three Conservative propositions (those on Empire First, building controls and the closed shop) were similarly accepted more often than they were rejected by Labour voters.

Agreement between voters for the two parties tended to be somewhat stronger on Conservative policies than on Labour. We have already mentioned the outstanding example of this—the support from Labour for a 'foreign policy based on "Empire First" '. In general, the Conservative propositions received a wider support than the Labour propositions. Conservatives accepted their own policies more often and their opponents' policies less often than Labour supporters did. However, the figures in Table 32 give no indication of how important individual items were felt to be, nor of the intensity of the emotions they aroused. It is possible, for example, that the lower average of support given by Labour voters to Labour statements was counterbalanced by stronger feelings over the question of employment than the Conservatives felt for any single one of their party's statements. It must be noted also that one of the principles on which items were selected—that their party origin should be readily identifiable, at least by the politically well-informed—meant that neither of the two selections could be regarded as including all the most important items of party policy. Indeed, as will be suggested in a later chapter, the method of selection may have led to the omission of some of the policies which were of most importance in gaining support for each party.

How far did self-described party supporters differ in their views on these issues from the 'followers'? Chiefly in the fact that party supporters, in whose lives politics played a more important part, and who were more familiar with the current language of political controversy, had more definite opinions than the followers. Followers gave many more 'don't know' answers than did supporters. Among supporters there was, on the average, little difference between Conservative and Labour in the proportion who had no opinion (for the ten statements the average proportion of 'don't know' answers was 14% for Conservative supporters and 13% for Labour supporters). But among the followers there was a considerable party (and hence class) difference. For all ten issues, the average proportion who were undecided was 19% for the Conservative followers, and 30% for Labour followers. The hint given here that politics and political issues are forced on the attention of most members of the middle class, whereas in the working class there are larger variations between those with different social roles (e.g., between men and women) and with different degrees of personal interest and commitment, is repeated frequently in our data.

The positive opinions of supporters and followers of the two parties are compared in Table 33. (Those with no opinion on each issue have been excluded from the percentage bases in this table. If this had not been done, the paradoxical results would have appeared that supporters were both more likely than followers to accept, and more likely also to reject some of the items.)

Greater commitment to one's party sharpens the differences of opinion between parties somewhat. Supporters were more likely to agree with the statements taken from the programme of their own party, and less likely to agree with those of the other party, than were the less active followers.[1] But these differences between supporters and followers were often fairly small, and, even among the party supporters, substantial groups accepted each of the proposals of their opponents. Party supporters differ from followers more in having opinions than in the content of those opinions.

We have seen that each of the ten policy statements on which we asked our informants' opinions was repudiated by a considerable number even of those who intended to vote for the party which fathered it. But we do not yet know how these criticisms were related to each other, whether disagreement with the parties tended to be deep but confined to a fairly narrow group of critics, or whether, on the other

[1] With the one exception of Labour voters' views on native self-government.

hand, most voters were inclined to jib at one or two of their party's pronouncements and accept the remainder. We shall therefore look at our informants' reception of the list of statements as a whole.

Table 33

DIFFERENCES OF OPINION BETWEEN PARTY SUPPORTERS AND PARTY FOLLOWERS

Vote intention	Conservative			Labour		
Party support	Sup-porter	Fol-lower	Total	Sup-porter	Fol-lower	Total
% agreeing with policy items*	%	%	%	%	%	%
Conservative						
State trading	96	91	94	40	51	45
Building controls	91	86	89	50	64	56
Closed shop	89	83	88	54	57	55
'Socialism'	86	79	83	26	29	28
Empire first	93	91	92	84	90	86
Labour						
Full employment	51	59	55	96	92	94
Workers' control	31	46	38	78	75	77
Equality	40	49	45	75	72	74
Nationalisation	5	10	8	70	52	61
Native self-government	51	55	53	77	82	79

* 'Don't Knows' for each item have been omitted when computing percentages.

In order to do this, replies to the ten questions have been combined into an Index of Political Opinion by the following method. Each Conservative answer (agreement with a Conservative statement, or disagreement with a Labour statement) was given a score of +1, each Labour answer a score of −1, and each 'don't know' answer a score of 0. When the scores are added, the resulting scale range from +10, representing agreement with the Conservative

10   145

point of view on all ten issues, to −10, representing agreement with Labour on all issues. A score of 0 represents a neutral position, which may include any number of 'don't know' answers, but in which each Conservative answer to an item is balanced by a Labour answer to another item. Table 34 shows how intending voters for the two major parties were distributed along this scale. Appropriate labels have been given to the divisions used.

Table 34

VOTE INTENTION AND POLITICAL OPINION SCORE

| | Vote intention | |
| | Conservative | Labour |
Political Opinion Score	%	%
Strongly Conservative (10–7)	24	1
Moderately Conservative (6–4)	38	4
Slightly Conservative (3–1)	21	16
Neutral (0)	10	17
Slightly Labour (−1 − −3)	7	30
Moderately Labour (−4 − −6)	—	25
Strongly Labour (−7 − −10)	—	7
N. (=100%)	(251)	(397)

Complete or near-complete acceptance of the official party outlook was rare among both groups of voters, but more Conservative than Labour voters approached it. About a quarter of the Conservatives, but fewer than 1 in 10 of the Labour voters agreed with their party spokesmen on 7 or more of the 10 issues. Almost two-thirds of the Conservatives are included in the groups we have called strongly Conservative and moderately Conservative (with scores of 4 or higher) but only about one third of the Labour voters are included in the similar groups on the Labour side of the scale, while almost 1 in 5 were placed in the neutral category, and a further 1 in 5 gave predominatingly Conservative answers.

We might be tempted to base on these last two figures a

lament about the ignorance and indifference of a large body of Labour voters towards all questions of general policy, and to conclude that their vote decision had been made in defiance of their own opinions. Such a conclusion, however, could not be justified without knowing something about the relative importance given to the opinions recorded, and the intensity of feeling with which they were held. Agreement with one's party on a single issue of over-riding importance might well outweigh disagreement over a host of lesser issues. We did not ask our informants how strongly they felt about the ten principles discussed here, but we did, in the second interview, obtain a measure of the relative importance they placed on a series of election issues. We showed them a list of eleven areas of controversy, with the comment 'The parties are arguing about these problems. Which would you say are the most important?' The replies are shown in Table 35.[1]

Two problems were given equally great importance by both parties—the cost of living and housing—but, after these, voters for the two parties differed, the Conservatives stressing nationalisation and taxation, and the Labour voters unemployment and the Health Service. These six problems together accounted for 83% of all replies. It is impossible to assess the respective contributions of political propaganda and personal experience to the relative stress given to the various issues. The cost of living and housing were certainly the dominant themes of Conservative electioneering. But they were also the only two matters mentioned with any frequency when we asked informants to name the most urgent problems facing them and their families at the time. (42%

[1] The information on which much of the remainder of this chapter and parts of the following chapters are based was obtained only from the 337 people whom we interviewed three times. This sub-sample was not designed to be strictly representative. Its composition is analysed in Appendix A, where it is shown that the chief differences between the sub-sample and the panel as a whole is that the former includes more people who were uncertain and changeable in their vote intention, a higher proportion of Conservatives, and a lower proportion of Labour voters than the panel as a whole. Since party choice is used as a control in all the following tables, the second difference is of little importance. The first difference may have affected the distribution of replies to our questions to some extent.

of the sample mentioned problems connected with the cost of living, and 28% housing difficulties.)

Table 35

MOST IMPORTANT ELECTION PROBLEMS

	Second Vote Intention	
	Conservative	Labour
Problems named	%	%
Cost of living	58	59
Housing	55	51
Nationalisation	39	20
Taxation	35	8
Unemployment	29	53
Food	18	23
Controls	17	9
Empire	16	7
Health Service	10	34
Profits	4	4
America	1	1
N. (=100%)	(123)	(166)

(Percentages add to more than 100% because up to three answers were recorded for each informant.)

The problems given first priority by electors of both parties were, in fact, those in which election speech-making and personal worries coincided. A similar coincidence probably accounts for the comparatively high frequency with which Labour voters named unemployment, and Conservative voters taxation. Nationalisation is the only one of the six frequently named issues which did not have an obvious and direct bearing on people's daily lives. Other issues whose impact on the individual were indirect were ignored. Comparatively few named 'controls' as an important issue, and fewer still, even among Labour voters, named 'profits'. 'America' is an oblique way of referring to a whole complex of problems : the dollar balance, Marshall Aid, foreign policy, control of atomic weapons, etc., and both parties have been criticised for playing down these issues in the 1950 election, but it is none the less surprising that only 1% in each party listed 'America' among the important problems of the election.

Finally, it may be noted that one problem—'food'—which would also appear to have an obvious and direct bearing on people's daily lives and which, through debates on subsidies, rationing and Government purchasing, was stressed by both parties in their campaigning, was given a comparatively low place in the list by both parties, although not as low as the more impersonal subjects, controls, profits and America. This suggests that the parties and the press may have been somewhat out of touch with public opinion in emphasising the food situation, but supports the view expressed above that the subjects considered most important were those where propaganda reinforced personal concern. Only 5% of the sample named food shortages and difficulties as the most urgent problem facing them and their families at the time.

Their dominant place in Conservative election propaganda may be one reason why Labour voters selected housing and the cost of living as two of the most important election issues. But this propaganda was totally unsuccessful in convincing them that the Conservative Party could deal with these problems better than the Labour Party could. We asked informants which party they thought was best able to handle each of four problems: housing, the cost of living, unemployment and Empire problems. The answers are shown in Table 36.

Answers to these questions were marked very strongly by party loyalty. In each case a majority named their own party as most capable of handling each of the problems—a majority that, with one exception, amounted to three-quarters or more of intending voters. The exception was not the same for Conservative voters as for Labour voters. Conservative voters were somewhat doubtful about their party's ability to prevent unemployment. Scarcely more than half named their own party, and although most of the remainder simply said they did not know, 18% named the Labour Party. Labour voters had no doubts about their party in regard to unemployment, but they did have them in regard to Empire

problems. Here again little more than half named their own
party, and 15% named the Conservative Party.

Table 36

VIEWS ON THE BEST PARTY TO HANDLE
CERTAIN PROBLEMS

*2nd Vote Intention**		*Problem*		
Conservative	*Cost of living*	*Housing*	*Unemployment*	*Empire*
% *replying*	%	%	%	%
Conservative	73	75	53	77
Labour	4	8	18	2
Liberal	2	1	1	2
Other parties	1	1	2	2
Don't know	20	15	26	17
N. (=100%)	(114)	(114)	(114)	(114)
Labour				
% *replying*				
Conservative	3	2	—	14
Labour	73	79	85	54
Liberal	—	—	—	1
Other parties	1	1	1	—
Don't know	23	18	14	31
N. (=100%)	(155)	(155)	(155)	(155)

* I.e. second time they were asked.

Unemployment, on the one side, and the Empire, on the
other, were not merely party themes in the 1950 election, but
have been for decades. Over a long period there has developed a tendency for opponents as well as supporters to con-
cede to each party unique gifts for handling the problem it
had particularly emphasised. It seems likely that this is not
merely a matter of attributing greater skill and knowledge
but also a greater degree of concern. Each party has developed a reputation for being concerned with a particular
problem sufficiently marked to counterbalance to some
extent the strong party loyalty which characterises answers
to most political questions. This is suggested not only by the

fact that some informants were prepared to name the rival party as most capable but also by the fact that others apparently said they didn't know which was most capable as a way of avoiding this admission. Conservatives gave more 'don't know' answers to the question on unemployment and Labour voters more to that on the Empire than to any others.

Housing and the cost of living, by contrast, were comparatively new problems. During the 1950 election campaign they were played up more by the Conservative than by the Labour Party, but both parties had a great deal to say about them. Moreover, although they differed in the methods they advocated for dealing with the problems, there was little to suggest to voters that either party felt a very much more serious concern with them than did the other. In any case, Table 36 shows that neither party had succeeded in 'capturing' the issues of housing and the cost of living, as the Labour Party had to some extent done with unemployment and the Conservative Party with Empire problems.

In a later chapter we shall suggest that this 'capturing' of certain problems by each party was of central importance in gaining and keeping for each a solid core of faithful voters. Other issues, for example, the reduction of taxation as a Conservative 'capture' could perhaps be added to the list. Unfortunately we have no information about the reputation of the parties among our informants on this score.

It may be pointed out that the replies to the questions on which party would do the best job for each class, discussed in Chapter 7, form a pattern similar to those on unemployment and the Empire. The majority answered these questions also by naming their own party, whichever it happened to be. But Labour voters were particularly strongly convinced that their party would do the best job for the working class, and this claim was conceded by a substantial minority of Conservative voters. Similarly, Conservative voters were particularly strongly convinced that their own party would do the best job for the middle class, and this claim was conceded by many Labour voters. Views on this much more general and vague issue show that here too there is evidence of a party reputation which cuts across specific political loyalties.

We have now seen something of what electors of both major parties thought on the issues of the election. Although opinions on the ten statements which we chose from the party programmes were markedly divided along political lines, there were in each case minorities who agreed with the opposition. The voters for the two parties agreed in naming housing and the cost of living as two of the most important problems, but they differed in the weight they gave to other problems. However, all thought that the party of their choice was the best fitted to handle the problems they considered most vital. In view of this, we may ask what people expected to happen after the election if the opposition party were returned. We asked our informants what they thought would happen if the Labour Government won the election, and if the Conservative Party won. The answers covered a wide range of hopes and fears, from 'Life won't be worth living', to 'Better conditions all round'. Most people indicated not only the kind of change they expected but the degree or intensity of change as well, and we have classified the answers by the degree of change expected. These answers are shown in Table 37.

Both parties expect much greater change from their opponents than from their friends. (It goes without saying that the adherents of each party expect the changes introduced by their own side to be good, and the changes introduced by their opponents to be bad.) The table seems to reflect a good deal of apprehensiveness about change. People are more ready to expect disaster than Utopia. Slight improvement is all that can be looked for, and fears are greater than hopes.

How far were expectations about which party would win the election influenced by these hopes and fears? Questions were asked about what informants thought would be the result of the election both in Greenwich and in Britain as a whole. The answers suggest that there was some wishful thinking, but that, at least as regards the result in Greenwich, where informants possessed more information on which to base their assessments of party chances, most people answered realistically. Replies are shown in Table 38.

Table 37

VIEWS ON THE CONSEQUENCES OF THE ELECTION

	1st Vote Intention	
Expectations	*Conservative*	*Labour*
	%	%
If Labour wins		
Marked change	50	8
Slight change	19	58
No change	12	15
Other answers	4	1
Don't know	15	18
If Conservatives win		
Marked change	17	52
Slight change	66	15
No change	2	5
Other answers	4	2
Don't know	11	26
N. (=100%)	(275)	(418)

Table 38

VIEWS ON THE PROBABLE RESULT OF THE ELECTION

	Vote Intention	
	Conservative	*Labour*
	%	%
Party expected to win in Greenwich		
Conservative	23	4
Labour	60	81
Don't know	17	15
Party expected to win throughout the country		
Conservative	45	5
Labour	24	67
Don't know	31	28
N. (=100%)	(275)	(418)

Voters for both parties agreed that Labour would win in Greenwich although Conservatives were less strongly convinced of this than were Labour voters. Both groups of voters showed much more reluctance to predict the result throughout the country. A majority of those who did attempt to predict it expected their own party to win, although again Conservatives were somewhat less confident about their chances of victory than were Labour voters.

It is a familiar feature of election speeches and election journalism that all parties exaggerate their own chances of victory. We might have expected that those who described themselves as party supporters would be more likely than the 'followers' to share this official optimism. But a comparison of the answers of supporters and followers does not support this speculation. Among those who intended to vote Labour, the followers were more likely than the supporters to say they did not know what would happen. But among those who gave a definite answer, neither party's supporters were more optimistic than its followers.

Chapter Ten

WHO WAS REACHED BY THE CAMPAIGN?

IN this chapter, the survey findings about the audience for different local campaign activities will be described, and the composite effectiveness of these activities in making the candidates known to the electorate discussed. We will give an account of the extent of listening to election broadcasts, and describe informants' habits and opinions towards other sources of political news and comment.

Of the different types of locally organised election propaganda described in Chapter Five, we questioned informants about three: election addresses, pamphlets and public meetings. None of these methods of presenting the party case had been striking enough to gain the attention or remain in the memory of even half of the electorate. Of the three, the election addresses had the widest audience; 40% of our sample had read at least one of them, while 28% had read at least one pamphlet, and only 7% had been to an election meeting.

Did the minorities who were reached in these ways pay attention only to the arguments put forward by their own side, or did they read those of both sides? Table 39 shows the political colour of their reading and attendance at meetings.

People pay more attention to the election propaganda of the party for which they intend to vote than they do to that of other parties, but comparatively large numbers (about two-thirds of the number who read their own party's case) also look at the arguments of the opposite party. But it can be

seen that hardly anyone, Conservative or Labour, read the
other party's case without also reading their own. (The percentage who read their own party's case plus those who read
none total almost 100% in each case.) The same thing is
true of attendance at meetings. Few went to meetings held
by the other party, and those who did were all members of
the little group who went to their own party's meetings. The
small band of Liberals appear to have been particularly
assiduous readers, though, being badly served by their own
party, they read Conservative and Labour addresses and
pamphlets more often than they read their own. None of
them went to meetings, however. At the other extreme,
those who had not made up their minds how they were going
to vote bothered least of all about reading the campaign
hand-outs. Few of them had any interest in politics and they
were in many respects the hardest group for the parties to
reach.

Table 39

ATTENTION TO ELECTION PROPAGANDA
AND VOTE INTENTION

Vote Intention

% reading election addresses of	Conservative %	Labour %	Liberal %	Don't know %
Conservatives	36	26	55	20
Labour	24	39	45	23
Liberals	10	7	35	11
None	60	57	45	73
Pamphlets of				
Conservatives	17	16	52	16
Labour	14	27	52	19
Liberals	6	6	24	5
None	77	71	33	79
% going to meetings of				
Conservatives	5	2	—	5
Labour	1	8	—	2
Liberals	1	—	—	2
None	95	92	100	95
	(127)	(131)	(21)	(57)

Who was reached by the Campaign?

The politically interested paid more attention to campaign propaganda than did the uninterested, but even among the 11% of the sample who said that they were very interested in politics, only about two-thirds read any of the election addresses, while among the 'not very interested' only 1 person in 4 read them. The proportions in each of the three interest groups who paid attention to local propaganda activities are shown in Table 40.

Table 40

ATTENTION TO ELECTION PROPAGANDA
AND INTEREST IN POLITICS

	Interest in Politics		
	Great	Moderate	Little
	%	%	%
% who			
Read election addresses	64	56	26
Read pamphlets	42	35	19
Attended meetings	16	11	5
N. (=100%)	(38)	(132)	(143)

We suggested in Chapter Five[1] that the main purpose of the local campaign, determined by the fact that no party affiliations appear on the ballot papers, was to impress the names of the candidates firmly on the minds of the electors. How far had this attempt succeeded by the time of our second interview? We must bear in mind that one of the candidates was the sitting member, and we have seen that about 1 person in 4 remembered his name at the time of our first interview.[2] In Table 41 we show the proportions who knew the names of each of the candidates at the time of our second interview.

People were more likely to know the name of the candidate for whom they intended to vote than that of the chief opposition candidate, though again the Liberals, particularly well informed about the other two names but not about

[1] Pp. 76-77.
[2] In spite of the unrepresentative composition of the second interview sample, the proportion who knew the name of their M.P. was the same as for the panel as a whole.

that of the Liberal candidate, were an exception. Within this general tendency, the Labour candidate Mr. Reeves was the best known. His supporters could give his name more often than the Conservatives could give that of his rival Mr. Gilbey, and, on the other hand, the Conservatives were considerably more likely to know the name of the Labour candidate than Labour voters were to know the name of the Conservative candidate. Nearly 9 out of 10 Labour supporters, about 8 out of 10 Conservatives and only about 4 out of 10 Liberals knew the names of their own party's candidates. Since there were still ten days of campaigning left when we began interviewing, and since there were doubtless some people who, although they could not recall their candidate's name when questioned, would nevertheless have recognised it on a ballot paper, it would seem that the two major parties had been fairly successful in making known the names of their candidates in spite of the lack of interest in their publications. They used, of course, other means besides those we have studied for achieving this end, the most important of which were probably posters and window cards.

Table 41

KNOWLEDGE OF CANDIDATES' NAMES

Vote Intention

% knowing name of candidate for	Conservative %	Labour %	Liberal %	Don't know %
Conservatives	79	52	90	56
Labour	75	88	95	74
Liberals	21	16	43	16

But if most people knew the name of their party's candidate, that was almost all they knew about him. When we asked, of each candidate, 'Do you happen to know what kind of a chap he is?', only about 3 out of 10 of our informants could offer any comment. (In the case of the Liberal candidate the proportion was only 3 in a 100.) People were more likely to know something about their own candidate than about his rival. (42% of these intending to vote Conservative offered some opinion about Mr. Gilbey, and 26% about Mr. Reeves. Of those intending to vote Labour, 16% gave an opinion about Mr. Gilbey, and 39% about Mr. Reeves.)

If the frequency of comments on the candidates suggests that there was little interest in them as individuals, the comments themselves suggest that they did not arouse any great emotion even among the minority who had something to say about them. Almost half of all the comments were non-committal snippets of biographical information. The worst that Labour voters could find to say about Mr. Gilbey was that he was 'not one of our class of people', while the Conservatives criticised Mr. Reeves as a politician rather than as a person. Praise for the voter's own candidate referred more often to his political abilities than to his personal virtues.

Our questions about the local campaign, then, indicate that neither the candidates nor their electioneering activities aroused much enthusiasm, but that, in spite of this, the party agents were reasonably successful in what, we have suggested, must be their main aim, to hammer home the names of their candidates.

The only part of the national campaign about which we asked detailed questions was the series of party election broadcasts, and even here our information is not as full and reliable as we would wish. It comes from two sources. In the first place, we asked each member of our sub-sample what political broadcasts they had listened to lately and who was the speaker. Since they were interviewed on different days while the election broadcasts were still in progress, not all informants had the same opportunities to listen. To remedy this shortcoming, we also conducted a separate daily poll, on the morning after each broadcast, using a quota sample of 100. The quotas were loosely controlled for sex and socio-economic status. Because of the pressure of other work, we were able to cover only 12 of the 14 broadcasts, and not all with a full quota of interviews. In Table 42 we give the results of these daily polls on broadcast listening.

Some supplementary information may be added from

these interviews. Many of those who listened did so with half an ear, for no more than an average of 26% claimed to have heard the whole broadcast. Half the listeners said they discussed the broadcasts afterwards with friends or members of the family.

Table 42

AUDIENCES FOR ELECTION BROADCASTS

Speaker	% who listened	No. in Sample
Winston Churchill	54	(100)
Charles Hill	46	(100)
Lord Woolton	43	(75)
Florence Horsbrugh	41	(82)
Anthony Eden	37	(95)
Clement Attlee	48	(75)
Herbert Morrison	46	(105)
Ernest Bevin	42	(125)
Margaret Herbison	41	(75)
Clement Davies	32	(100)
Lady M. Lloyd George	32	(98)
Harry Pollitt	20	(75)

When we compare our Greenwich results with the national audience figures released by the BBC Listener Research department, it would appear that Greenwich audiences were in general larger than the average audience for the whole country, though the differences vary from speaker to speaker.[1] In particular, our figures are generally higher for the Labour speakers—where the national average for these was 36%, the Greenwich average was 43%. In a predominantly Labour constituency an even larger difference might have been expected, but, such as it is, the variation is almost certainly a reflection of local colour.

To find out more about these radio audiences we must return to our sub-sample. Incomplete as our figures are, they make it clear that as a whole the election broadcasts attracted a much wider audience than any part of the local campaign. 69% of our sample (the real figure may have been higher)

[1] See H. G. Nicholas: *The British General Election of 1950*, p. 127.

remembered listening to at least one election broadcast—almost twice as many as the number who read any of the election addresses, and ten times the number who found their way to election meetings.

Probably the most striking thing about these broadcast audiences was their political range. Unlike audiences for other types of campaign propaganda, listeners were not drawn primarily to the spokesmen of their own party. Mr. Churchill was, irrespective of vote intention, the most popular speaker among all groups; Mr. Attlee was heard by almost equal proportions of Conservative and Labour voters; Dr. Charles Hill drew more listeners among people who intended to vote Labour than any Labour Party speaker except Mr. Attlee. On the average, only 43% of those who listened to speakers for the two major parties were in political sympathy with them; the rest were opponents or undecided. This success in obtaining hearers from all sides was more marked in the case of the party leaders (and of Dr. Hill who, as the Radio Doctor, had already built up popularity as a broadcaster) than of other speakers.

Another striking feature of the broadcasts is that, unlike other forms of propaganda, they reached those who were undecided about how they would vote as much as the decided voters. 67% of the 'don't knows' had listened to at least one broadcast, compared with 70% of those with Conservative and 64% of those with Labour vote intentions.

Those who described themselves as interested in politics listened more often than the uninterested, and here there was a considerable party (and hence class) difference. 79% of interested Conservative voters, and 84% of interested Labour voters heard at least one broadcast. Uninterested Conservative voters paid less attention—only 62% of them heard any of the speeches, but this proportion was very much higher than that among the uninterested Labour voters. More than half these last did not listen to any of the broadcasts (44% listened to at least one), and not even Mr. Churchill drew a large audience. This difference provides further support for a conclusion suggested earlier, that in the middle class all groups are induced by the patterns of culture to pay some attention to politics, whereas in the working class some groups (women and the uninterested) can remain comparatively cut off from political thought and discussion. Our survey provides little more than a number of hints at this conclusion, but the variations in interest in both classes provide a problem worth studying in the future.

We also asked informants whether they had seen the newsreel items of the three party leaders. Only 2 people out of 10 had seen any of them. This proportion did not vary much with vote intention. Conservatives were slightly less likely to have seen them, but they reached the 'don't knows' as often as they reached Labour voters. There was no tendency for people to have seen (or to recall) the film of their own party leader more than the others.

We were not able to make any detailed study of the reading of election news in the daily press, and as newspaper reading has been studied extensively and with much larger samples than ours, we will deal with it very briefly. Only 16 of our 337 informants reported that they were buying more newspapers than usual during the election. The papers read by those who voted for one of the major parties are shown in Table 43. The figures refer to papers read on the day preceding our interview. Newspaper reading habits are strongly associated with class differences. Since we obtained information about newspapers read only from our second interview sample, to introduce a class control is to reduce some of the totals to very small numbers. We have, however, included this double breakdown in addition to the totals for Conservative and Labour voters, although the figures must be regarded as giving only a very rough indication.

If we look first at the newspapers read by Conservatives and Labour voters as a whole, we see that most people read a paper of their own political complexion. (The papers differed in the extent and openness of their party support but, not to make unduly fine distinctions, the *Express*, *The Times* and *Telegraph*, and *Mail* may be regarded as Conservative, and the *Mirror* and *Herald* as Labour. The *News Chronicle* supported the Liberals.) The most popular papers among Labour voters were the *Mirror* and the *Herald*;

Who was reached by the Campaign?

among Conservative voters the *Express*, *The Times*, *Telegraph* and the *Mirror*, the paper which most strongly cut across party allegiances (and which, according to Mr. H. G. Nicholas's analysis of election news in the daily press during the 1950 campaign, 'was the most wary of all the national papers in admitting election material to its pages . . .').

Table 43

VOTE, CLASS AND NEWSPAPER READING

1950 Vote Self-assigned Class	Conservative			Labour		
	Middle %	*Working* %	*Total** %	*Middle* %	*Working* %	*Total** %
% reading						
Daily Express	45	40	44	35	13	17
Daily Mirror	21	38	28	61	59	59
The Times or Daily Telegraph	36	7	24	2	4	2
Daily Mail	22	14	19	—	6	6
News Chronicle	10	10	10	30	12	14
Daily Herald	4	12	7	39	39	39
Other	7	12	12	9	4	3
None	4	10	6	9	10	9
N. (=100%)	(67)	(42)	(115)	(23)	(140)	(172)

* Includes those who could not name their own class.

The papers read most by Conservatives are also those most read by the middle class generally, and similarly those read by Labour voters are those read by the working class. When we consider class and vote differences together we can see that both politics and class influence the choice of paper. There seem to be three different patterns of choice. Firstly, some papers are read much more by one of the four socio-political groups than by the other three. *The Times* and *Telegraph* are read mainly by middle-class Conservatives; the *News Chronicle* more frequently by middle-class Labour voters than by others (the *News Chronicle* is the nearest approach among those included in Table 43 to a middle-class Labour paper, in that it was at least not pro-Conservative). Then

163

there are papers which are read by three groups more than by the remaining group. Working-class Labour voters are the only group which does not read the *Daily Express* fairly frequently; the *Daily Mirror* drops to fourth place only among middle class Conservatives (although still read by 1 in 5 of them). Finally, there are papers whose readership is biassed more strongly by politics than by class. The *Daily Herald*, the only official party paper in our list, is the chief example of this type. It is second to the *Daily Mirror* in readership among Labour voters of both classes, but is little read by Conservatives of either class. The *Daily Mail* is read more by Conservatives of both classes than by Labour voters.

Although, with the resources available, we were not able to measure the reading of election news in the daily press, we do know that when informants were asked where they got their information about politics, the largest number of references was to newspapers. The detailed replies to this question have already been given (see above p. 137). There is no need to repeat them here, because the proportions mentioning each source did not vary greatly with vote, although Conservatives tended to name a slightly larger number of sources. Of the sample as a whole, 72% mentioned newspapers, 62% radio, and 46% talking to people. However, the radio was regarded as a more reliable source of news than the press. 40% thought radio and 23% thought newspapers the most reliable source.

Informants were also asked whether there were any newspapers they particularly trusted or particularly distrusted about politics. The answers are shown in Table 44.

Whether because they felt they lacked standards of judgment or because they were insufficiently familiar with papers other than their own, or because they thought all papers were on the same level, a large number of voters for each party did not name a paper in reply to these questions. But among those who replied, the papers most trusted by voters for one party tended to be those most distrusted by voters for the other, although *The Times* and *Daily Telegraph* have achieved a sufficiently august reputation to be exempt from distrust, and neither party trusted the *Daily Worker*.

Table 44

NEWSPAPERS TRUSTED AND DISTRUSTED

	Papers trusted		Papers distrusted	
Vote intention	Conservative	Labour	Conservative	Labour
	%	%	%	%
Daily Telegraph	18	2	1	1
Daily Express	17	3	1	5
News Chronicle	8	5	*	1
Daily Mail	6	1	2	8
The Times	5	4	—	—
Daily Mirror	2	9	13	4
Daily Herald	1	17	16	2
Daily Worker	*	2	15	4
None	39	54	54	67
N. (=100%)	(277)	(418)	(277)	(418)

* Less than 1%
Percentages add to less than 100 because some informants name paper not listed here.

Two general trends emerge from the figures discussed in this chapter. The case in favour of each party, whether put forward officially (election addresses, pamphlets, public meetings) or unofficially (in the daily press), tended to reach those who had already decided to vote for that party more than those who opposed it; and both sides were listened to much more by the most strongly committed section of the voters, the politically interested, than by the uninterested and undecided. The medium which most nearly overcame these two tendencies was radio. The party broadcasts provided the nearest approach to personal contact with the political leaders, and this broke down to some extent both the habit of the committed of listening primarily to their own party, and the isolation of the uninterested. But there remained a substantial number among those with little interest in politics (tending to belong, economically, to the lower ranks of society, and more often women than men) who ignored even the broadcasts.

Although we were unable to get detailed information about the reading of election news in the daily press, the difference between interested and uninterested seems likely to be even greater here than for radio broadcasts. (The interested named newspapers as a source of political information considerably more often than they named radio; the uninterested named the two sources equally often. See p. 137 above.) Nor did the uninterested compensate for their insulation from the formal media through personal contacts. About half of them could not recall taking part in any political discussion during three or four weeks (p. 135); few of them thought of 'talking to people' as a source of political information. Indeed the political information of many seems to have been extremely rudimentary. Barely half of the politically uninterested were able to name even the party of the member who represented them in Parliament.

With the spread of television some of this information about the section of the electorate which active party workers have long recognised as posing their greatest problems may have ceased to be of any but historical interest. If in 1950 radio was the most successful means of bringing politics to the unpolitical, television in the future seems likely to be even more successful. These figures from the pre-television era may comfort those whose first reaction is to deplore its growing influence even more than those who welcome it.

Chapter Eleven

TYPES OF CHANGE IN VOTE INTENTION

I N previous chapters the political alignments of the Greenwich electors as they were on Polling Day, 23rd February, 1950, were examined. We saw that choice of party is associated not only with opinions on the issues of the election but also with such stable sociological characteristics as socio-economic status, sex and age. These facts suggest, as everyday experience does also, that political allegiances change infrequently. But the device of the panel survey enables us to go beyond inference and unsystematic common-sense observation and find out how much change of opinion in fact occurred in the period covered by our fieldwork. We now turn back from election day to the campaign period which preceded it, to ask what shifts of allegiance took place, who were the people who changed their minds, and what evidence we can find of the reasons and influences which lead to change.

Firstly, to what extent were the vote intentions expressed to interviewers on December 1949 followed out on election day? This is shown in Table 45.

A comparison of the overall distribution of vote intentions given in December with votes recorded in February (these figures are shown in the marginal columns) suggests that very little change had taken place. The Labour vote had increased by 3%, and the non-voters were 3% fewer than the initially undecided. Conservative and Liberal shares of the electorate had changed even less. These are the changes which would have been shown by two successive cross-sectional polls of the familiar kind. But since in our survey the two interviews were taken with the same people, we can see that the amount of change was considerably higher than these total figures suggest. In all, 22% of our sample changed their minds, and there were changes in every possible direction: from Conservative to Labour as well as from Labour to Conservative, from indecision to Liberal and from Liberal to non-voting, etc.

Table 45

CHANGES IN VOTE DECISION BETWEEN
DECEMBER 1949 AND FEBRUARY 1950

Vote Intention December 1949

	Conservative	Labour	Liberal	Don't know	Total
	%	%	%	%	%
1950 Vote					
Conservative	83	3	19	16	31
Labour	7	88	23	62	57
Liberal	4	3	46	6	5
Did not vote	6	6	12	16	7
N. (=100%)	(245)	(395)	(26)	(70)	(736)
Vote intention as % of total	32	54	4	10	100

The movement during the campaign period was in favour of Labour, who increased their share of the total vote by 3%, while the Conservative share diminished slightly. The bulk of Labour gains came from those who originally said they did not know how they would vote. The 'don't knows' made up 11% of the eventual Labour vote, and only 5% of the Conservative vote. But the Labour Party also gained votes directly from the Conservatives. Although there was a two-way exchange of voters between the Conservative and Labour Parties, the balance was in the Labour Party's favour.

These changes may seem surprising in an election which decreased the Labour margin not only throughout the country but also in Greenwich. But if we look back to 1945, we can see that Labour was only winning back, during the campaign period, part of what it had lost during the inter-election years.[1] Exactly half of the 68 persons who changed to Labour during the campaign had voted Labour in 1945, but had apparently had doubts, at the time of our December interview, as to whether they would continue to vote Labour in 1950. On the other hand, only 5 of the small group of 27 who changed to Conservative during the campaign had already voted Conservative in 1945. Moreover, those who did switch from Conservative to Labour between the two elections made up their minds at the last moment during the campaign period, whereas those who changed from Labour to Conservative had almost all decided on the change by December. The balance of changes of allegiance between 1945 and 1950 was in favour of the Conservatives.

The small group of Liberals in our sample was particularly inconstant. Less than half of those who gave a Liberal intention in December finally voted Liberal, while of those who intended to vote for one of the major parties 4 out of 5 eventually did so. On the other hand, those who finally voted Liberal decided on their vote later than did the Conservative and Labour voters. Only 32% of the eventual Liberal voters announced a Liberal intention in December, but 88% of Conservative voters and 84% of Labour voters correctly forecast their own votes. The remaining 7 out of 10 Liberal voters consisted of 3 former Conservatives, 3 former Labour intenders, and 1 who had been uncertain. The instability of the Liberal vote suggests that, at least in Greenwich (where there had not been a Liberal candidate since 1935, and no continuous local party organisation for an even longer period), many people voted Liberal more out of dissatisfaction or indifference about their own party than out of positive conviction.

Because the numbers who changed from any one party to any other were in all cases small, further discussion of how such changes contributed to the fortunes of the parties would be worth little. But the types of change can be classified without reference to the particular parties involved. In

[1] An analysis of change between the two elections is given in Appendix D.

the following pages we shall divide informants into five groups:

Constants — Those whose party choice remained unchanged from one interview to the next.

Crystallisers — Those who changed from indecision to a definite choice of party.

Converts — Those who switched from one party to another.

Disintegrators — Those who started out with a definite vote intention which later dissolved into indecision or non-voting.

Indifferents — Those who had no party choice at either interview.

For the panel as a whole, a classification into these groups can be based on December vote intention and February vote, as recorded in the post-poll interview. The proportions in each group are shown in Table 46.

Table 46

TYPES OF OPINION CHANGE BETWEEN
DECEMBER 1949 AND POLLING DAY

	%
Constants	77
Crystallisers	8
Converts	8
Disintegrators	6
Indifferents	1
N. (=100%)	(736)

Almost everybody committed himself to a party at some time, if in some cases after hesitating (the crystallisers), and in others ineffectually (the disintegrators). Only about 1 in 100 failed to name the party for which he thought of voting or failed to vote. Over three-quarters of the sample announced their party allegiance in December and kept it unchanged on polling day. Of those who did change, the majority (14% of the sample—the crystallisers and disintegrators) never

allied themselves to more than one party. Finally, 8%
switched parties at some time in the eight weeks between
our two interviews.

There are interesting features about these figures, the most
striking of which is perhaps the rarity of complete indifference. Although, as we have seen, many people felt little interest in the election, few felt it to be so completely remote
from them that they never expressed a preference for any
party. But most of the figures in Table 45 rest on an arbitrary
basis. The proportion of constants can be regarded as a
maximum figure, and those for different types of change as
minimum estimates since, if more interviews had been made
with each informant, or if the first interview had been either
closer to or further away from election day, the proportions
in the different groups would certainly have changed.

Some idea of what these changes might have been can be
gained by studying the selected group of informants whom
we interviewed during the fortnight preceding the election.
This sub-sample included a rather higher proportion of
changers than did the panel as a whole, and accordingly, as
a base for comparison, we give in Table 47 firstly the changes
over the whole period of our survey, and then the intermediate changes, between December and the pre-poll interview,
and between the pre-poll and the post-poll interviews.

Between the December interview (before the date of the
election had been announced) and the pre-poll interview
(during the last fortnight of the campaign) changes of
opinion were characterised by increasing commitment. Most
of those who in December did not know how they would vote
had, by the time of our pre-poll interview, made a decision,
and few of those with a vote intention in December had
'disintegrated' into uncertainty. During the latter part of the
campaign period the largest group of changes were from
one party to another. A handful of these last-minute changes
were made by people who had left their original party, but
returned to it on polling day. (In panel-survey terminology,
the 'waverers'.) But most of them were genuine changes,
made by people who had twice announced their intention
of voting for one party, but who finally voted for a different

party. Unfortunately, we do not know how close to polling day these conversions occurred, but well over half of those who definitely changed parties between December and election day changed *after* our campaign interview.

Table 47

TYPES OF OPINION CHANGE BETWEEN
SUCCESSIVE INTERVIEWS

Interviews on which distribution based	Changes over entire survey period	Intermediate changes	
	December to post-poll	December to pre-poll	Pre-poll to post-poll
	%	%	%
Types of change			
Constants	71	75	80
Crystallisers	13	13	6
Converts	10	6	8
Disintegrators	4	2	5
Indifferents	2	4	1
N. (=100%)	(326)	(326)	(326)

From the fact that in Table 47 the percentage for change between successive interviews total more than the percentage of change between December and election day, it can be seen that some people changed more than once. There was, in fact, some tendency for changes to be concentrated in the replies of a few individuals. Those who changed their minds between the first and second interviews were more likely than those who remained constant, to change during the last fortnight of the campaign. (33% of the former group and 13% of the latter group changed during the last fortnight of the campaign.) Nevertheless, when all three interviews are taken into account, only 67% of our second-interview sample (somewhat less stable in its opinions than the panel as a whole) remained constant to one party throughout.

A sixth group of changers has been mentioned above in passing—the 'waverers', who at some time before the election abandoned their original vote intention, but finally returned to it. In the Sandusky survey, the pioneer American study of the present type, one finding about the 'waverers' was that 'if a person leaves his party for indecision he almost always returns to it later, but if he leaves it for the opposition, he seldom returns to it.'[1] Few waverers could be identified from the Greenwich data (although we would doubtless have found more if we had been able to make more interviews with each informant). However, the American finding does seem to be confirmed by the small group in our sample. Of the 20 people who switched, between the first two interviews, from their original party to another party, only 4 returned to it on polling day; of the 7 who wavered from their original choice to indecision, 5 returned on polling day. A similar difference is found if we look at those who, in the December interview, wavered from the party for which they voted in 1945. Of the 52 people who gave as their vote intention a party other than the one for which they had voted in 1945 only 14 (27%) returned on polling day to their 1945 party. But of the 37 people who had voted in 1945 but said in our December interview that they did not know how they would vote in 1950, 26 (70%) returned on polling day to the party for which they had previously voted.[2] Changing parties, even in an opinion poll interview, appears to be a serious matter. Most of those who announce a change stick to it.

Conversions, or switches from one party to another, were less common than changes which involved only one party—from uncertainty to choice, and from choice to uncertainty or non-voting. Whatever combination of interviews we consider, and whether we look at the whole panel or only at the sub-sample, the ratio is roughly the same. For every 4 people who changed parties, 6 swung between the one party of their choice and uncertainty.

The above analysis of the replies of the sub-sample whom

[1] Paul F. Lazarsfeld, Bernard Berelson and Hazel Gaudet, *The People's Choice*, New York, 1948, p. 66. Our classification of types of change is a modification of that used in this survey.
[2] These figures are based on the total sample.

we interviewed three times has confirmed the suggestion that the figure of 22% for the proportion of the total sample who changed their minds about their vote intention during the ten-week period of our survey is probably an understatement. However, in our discussion of change in the following chapters we will use data from the entire panel wherever possible, since the sample is larger and more nearly representative.

Chapter Twelve

WHO WERE THE CHANGERS?

I N the previous chapter we discussed the amount of change in party allegiance that occurred between our first interview in December 1949 and polling day in February 1950, and distinguished a number of different types of change. 22% of the sample changed their minds about how they would vote, but less than half of these switched from one party to another. These 'converts' were equalled in number by the 'crystallisers', who at first did not know how they would vote; a third, and only slightly smaller group, were the 'disintegrators', who at first had a definite party choice but failed to go to the polls. Only 1% of the sample expressed no party preference at any stage.

Doubtless our figure of 22% does not include all who changed their intentions at some time during the campaign, since we were not on hand to record all periods of doubt or temporary conversion. Analysis of the sub-sample with whom an intermediate interview was taken suggests that the percentage of changes would be somewhat higher had more interviews been taken, but that a considerable body who stayed constant to one party would have remained.

So far, only the amount and type of change has been studied. We have learnt nothing of the kind of people who change. Are some more likely than others to hesitate before making up their minds, to change parties, or to fail to vote?

The answer to this question is bound up with two main sets of factors, the first of which is interest in politics. We have already seen that people who are interested in politics are

175

more likely to follow out their vote intention on polling day than are those with little interest in politics. In Table 48, electors with different degrees of interest are grouped according to our classification of types of change.[1]

Table 48

TYPES OF CHANGE AND INTEREST IN POLITICS

Type of change	Great or Moderate %	Little %
Constants	83	70
Converts	7	9
Crystallisers	5	11
Disintegrators	4	8
Indifferents	1	2
N. (=100%)	(369)	(360)

Those who are more interested are also more constant, largely because they hesitate less before making up their minds and they seldom fail to vote. But they appear to be also slightly less likely than the uninterested to change parties.

The above table is based on the general question which we asked in our December interview about 'interest in politics'. Since the relationship which it shows between lack of interest and change, although consistent, is small, we show in Table 49 the answers given by each change group when we asked, in the second interview, about their interest in the General Election.

The greatest interest in the election was expressed by the constants, and the least by the non-voters, while the converts and the crystallisers were between these two extremes. The numbers on which percentages are based are small, and the differences are not statistically significant, but the trend is the same as that shown in Table 48.

Another series of questions is relevant to the relationship between interest and change. The interested were much more likely than the uninterested to have read the campaign

[1] These are defined above, p. 170.

literature, and to have listened to party election broadcasts. Which of the change groups read and heard the most of these official electioneering activities? The answers are given in Table 50.

Table 49

TYPES OF CHANGE AND INTEREST IN THE GENERAL ELECTION

Interest	Change group			
in Election	Constant	Convert	Crystallise	Did not vote
	%	%	%	%
Great	46	28	28	5
Moderate	38	34	30	43
Little	16	38	42	52
N. (=100%)	(231)	(32)	(44)	(21)

Table 50

TYPES OF CHANGE AND ATTENTION GIVEN TO CAMPAIGN PROPAGANDA

	Change group			
	Constant	Convert	Crystallise	Did not vote
	%	%	%	%
% who				
Read election addresses	45	34	20	20
Read party pamphlets	29	31	16	25
Went to meetings	8	—	—	—
Listened to party broadcasts	70	78	64	52
N. (=100%)	(231)	(32)	(44)	(21)

It is clear that non-voters and the people who at first had no definite vote intention paid less attention to any of the campaign activities than did the constants and the people who changed parties. Indecision appears, from this series of tables, to be much more often the result of indifference than of serious and questioning doubt. The differences between the constants and the converts are not always consistent (the small group of converts in our sample read election addresses less often, but read party pamphlets and listened to election broadcasts slightly more often than did the constants), but there is little positive evidence to suggest that the converts followed the arguments put forward by the parties more assiduously than did the constants.

The nature of audiences at political meetings is, at least, quite clear: the only people to attend them were the politically constant. Although, as we have seen, a few people went to meetings held by parties other than their own, no one changed allegiances as a result of the experience. This does not, of course, imply that political meetings have no useful function at election times. If no converts are made through them, they may have helped to reinforce convictions, to provide the faithful with facts and arguments they could use in support of their cause, and to give them the feeling that they were doing something to help it.

Interest in politics is, we have seen, associated with sex (men are more interested than women), with social status (the middle class are more interested than the working class), with years at school (those who continued their formal education after 14 were more interested than those who left school at 14), and with union membership (union members were more interested than employed persons who were not union members). But of these variables only sex shows a regular relationship with all types of change. Women make up their minds later than men, change parties more often, and more often fail to vote. Age, however, is also associated with change. Those aged fifty and over changed more often than those under fifty. The percentages of men and women, old and young, who changed their minds are shown in Table 51.

There is no such simple and regular relationship between change and social class, or attributes closely associated with social class, such as education, or trade union membership. Those on the lowest socio-economic level (our 'D' grade) were more likely than others to fail to vote, but they were not more likely to change parties, nor even to be slower in reaching a decision about how to vote. But when we take into account also the vote intention of our informants, a very clear pattern emerges. People whose vote intention is the same as that of the majority of their group (i.e. conformist) are highly likely to stick to it on polling day. Those with a deviant vote intention (i.e. one which differs from that of the

Table 51

TYPES OF CHANGE AMONG SEX AND AGE GROUPS

	Sex		Age	
	M.	F.	Under 50	50 and over
	%	%	%	%
Constant	82	72	80	71
Convert	7	9	7	9
Crystallise	7	9	7	10
Disintegrate	3	8	5	8
Indifferent	1	2	1	2
N. (=100%)	(325)	(393)	(469)	(254)

majority of their group) are less likely to remain constant to it, more likely to change to another party, and more likely to be non-voters. This is true for a variety of characteristics— socio-economic status, subjective class assessment, occupation, union membership, education—which are alike in denoting social groups whose members tend to share a common political outlook. The differences between conformists and deviants are shown in Table 52.

A member of the middle class who intended, ten weeks before the election, to vote Labour was much more likely to change to another party by election day than was his social equal who intended to vote Conservative. Similarly a member of the working class who intended to vote Conservative was more likely to switch parties than were his numerous equals who intended to vote Labour. The two deviant groups were also more likely than the conformists to fail to vote (although the differences are smaller than in the case of

179

Table 52*

CHANGES OF OPINION AMONG THOSE WITH
CONFORMIST AND DEVIANT VOTE INTENTIONS

(a) *S.E.S.*

Vote intention	Av.+ and Av.		Av.— and D	
	Conservative	Labour	Conservative	Labour
	%	%	%	%
1950 Vote				
Same as V.I.	91	80	78	89
Other party	6	16	15	5
Did not vote	3	4	7	6
N. (=100%)	(95)	(25)	(148)	(362)

(b) *Self-assigned class*

Vote intention	Middle		Working	
	Conservative	Labour	Conservative	Labour
	%	%	%	%
1950 Vote				
Same as V.I.	88	75	76	91
Other party	8	17	14	4
Did not vote	4	8	10	5
N. (=100%)	(145)	(88)	(42)	(330)

(c) *Hall-Jones Occupation Grade*

Vote intention	1–4		5–7	
	Conservative	Labour	Conservative	Labour
	%	%	%	%
1950 Vote				
Same as V.I.	95	64	71	92
Other party	4	22	16	4
Did not vote	1	14	13	4
N. (=100%)	(78)	(14)	(134)	(337)

* The bases for percentages in this table are seldom as large as would be desirable, and many of the differences are not statistically significant. However, the results gain force from the consistency with which the pattern reappears.

Who Were the Changers?

(d) Union Membership

Vote intention	Non-member†		Member	
	Conservative	Labour	Conservative	Labour
	%	%	%	%
1950 Vote				
Same as V.I.	87	88	82	90
Other party	7	7	14	5
Did not vote	6	5	4	5
N. (=100%)	(97)	(88)	(49)	(174)

(e) School-leaving age

Vote intention	15 and over		14 and under	
	Conservative	Labour	Conservative	Labour
	%	%	%	%
1950 Vote				
Same as V.I.	91	83	76	89
Other party	6	13	16	4
Did not vote	3	4	8	7
N. (=100%)	(102)	(55)	(141)	(339)

† Those not working have been omitted.

change of parties). Class position by itself has little relationship to change. Nor, perhaps surprisingly, have years of schooling. Among those whose vote intention was Conservative, the electors who left school at 14 or less were the more likely to change; among those intending to vote Labour, change was more frequent among people whose schooling continued beyond 14. Again it is the deviants who are most likely to change.

The effect of trade union membership is a particularly striking confirmation of the operation of group pressures. Informants who were working but did not belong to a trade union were almost evenly divided in their political preferences between the two major parties. They belonged to all socio-economic levels, had a wide variety of jobs, and cannot, even in the loosest sense, be described as belonging to a common social group. Among them, there was no difference in the amount of change between those intending to vote Conservative and those intending to vote Labour. But among union members, a majority of whom vote Labour, those who intended to vote Conservative and against the majority were the more likely to change.

We have provisionally used the phrase 'group pressure' to account for the fact that people whose vote intention differs from that of the majority of their 'group' are more likely to change their minds than are those whose vote intention conforms to that of the majority. But social classes, occupational strata, the trade union movement, the better educated and the less well educated are social groups only in a rather indirect sense. People do tend to associate more closely, through family, friends and formal organisations, with those who belong on the same social level as themselves than they do with their superiors or inferiors. But a given individual has personal contact with only a minute fraction of those we have here described as members of his 'group'. We have, indeed, no evidence that a single one of our informants was personally acquainted with any of the others. Our argument rests on the assumption that they did have relatives, friends and acquaintances within their own groups (as defined by our indices), and that these associates shared the political outlook of the group.

However, we do have some evidence of the vote intentions of people with whom our informants were in close social contact—in other words, of members of the same primary groups. In the December interview we asked informants whether there was anyone in their family, living in the same house, who was going to vote differently from them; and in the pre-poll interview we asked them to think of the three persons with whom they worked most closely at their job, and of their three closest friends outside work. We then asked them how each of these friends and co-workers intended to vote. Table 53 compares the amount of change among those whose families were unanimously of their own political opinion with the amount among people living in families with divided political allegiances, and among people who did not know how all their family members were going to

Who Were the Changers?

vote. Similar comparisons are made with regard to the vote
intentions of the first friend and the first co-worker named
by the informant.

Table 53

CHANGES OF OPINION AMONG THOSE IN POLITI-
CAL AGREEMENT AND DISAGREEMENT WITH
FAMILY AND ASSOCIATES*

	Anyone in family voting differently?		
	No	*Yes*	*Don't know*
Informant's 1950 vote	%	%	%
Same as V.I.	88	70	78
Other party	6	25	18
Did not vote	6	5	4
N. (=100%)	(489)	(83)	(68)

	Friend's vote intention		
	Same as own	*Different*	*Don't know*
Informant's vote	%	%	%
Same as V.I.	91	74	79
Other party	5	20	13
Did not vote	4	6	8
N. (=100%)	(187)	(50)	(52)

	Co-worker's vote intention†	
	Same as own	*Different*
Informant's vote	%	%
Same as V.I.	93	77
Other party	3	18
Did not vote	4	5
N. (=100%)	(106)	(44)

* The informant's vote intention at the time when the question about how
others intended to vote was asked has been used in each case. For the table
showing family's vote, this was the December vote intention; for the remaining
tables it was the vote intention given in the second interview. Degrees of change
in the last two parts of the table cannot therefore be directly compared with
those in the first part or in preceding tables. Not only had opinions moved
nearer to their final distribution by the second interview but a part only of the
original sample was interviewed.

† The number of cases in which informants did not know how their co-
worker would vote is too small for inclusion.

183

How People Vote

The differences shown in this table are striking. Of the people who lived in households where all family members intended to vote in the same way only 1 in 16 changed to another party. Of those living in families where at least one member intended to vote differently, 1 in 4 switched parties. It is true that we had no direct evidence of how other family members intended to vote. We had to rely on our informants' reports, and these may have been distorted by their own desires and prejudices; but they were more likely to over-estimate than to under-estimate the political unity of their families. Such a bias in the answers would conceal rather than sharpen the differences in amount of change between those whose families were divided and those where they were in agreement. People whose friends or co-workers had a different vote intention from themselves were also more likely to change than those whose associates were in political harmony with them.

The political opinions of family, friends and associates at work have, then, a more powerful influence on how people vote than any of the factors we have so far examined. We do not, however, know the mechanism by which this influence operated. Did family and friends convert the black sheep through direct and open argument about the merits of parties and policies? Was the discussion calmly rational, or were sanctions brought to bear to compel conformity? If there were sanctions, how strong were they—teasing and ridicule, or hostile silences and black looks at the dinner table, or angry recrimination? Or were the changes made under influences less overt and declared? Where family and friends had different vote intentions, the potential convert saw another political point of view presented in familiar circumstances, and an opposing attitude may have lost its terrors and gained warmth through the affection or respect felt for its supporter. Or again, the mechanism of conversion may have been a negative one. Families and groups of friends who agreed politically enjoyed the sense of sharing a common cause, and helped to reinforce each other's convictions. The mere absence of mutual support may have led to lukewarm conviction and vacillation.

184

Who Were the Changers?

We have singled out for comment the groups most likely to change, but we might equally well have emphasised the groups most likely to remain constant to their original intentions. Looked at from this side, the conclusion arising from the preceding tables might well be that the knowledge of agreement with fellow members of his group, whether family, circle or friends, or colleagues at work, further strengthens a person's already strong inclination to stand by his established convictions.

It is to be hoped that future research will help to answer these questions. Meanwhile, everyday experience suggests that conversions through open argument, while they undoubtedly occur sometimes, are comparatively infrequent, and that social groups move towards unanimity through much more indirect means—for example, through the suggestive power of the implicit assumption of agreement which forms a background to much political discussion, and is accompanied by hostile references to the supporters of opposing parties, giving a veiled threat of ostracism if the listener should be one of them.

The data so far presented in this chapter suggest that at least two factors are associated with change of opinion: interest in politics, and group attitudes. Those least interested in politics appear to be the most likely to change their minds. Secondly, those who differ from the majority of people of similar status, and from their family and associates are the most likely to change. Before going on to discuss other factors, it is worthwhile pausing to consider the relationship between interest and conformity. Are these two forces merely different aspects of the one thing? Are the interested more likely to conform to their group norms, and the uninterested more likely to deviate? In Table 54 we compare the votes of interested and uninterested within each broad socio-economic level.

Political conformity and interest in politics do not appear to be related. The uninterested in both classes more often fail to vote, but when they do vote their choice of party is very similar to that of the interested.

Table 54

INTEREST IN POLITICS AND CONFORMITY
TO CLASS VOTE

Interest in Politics	S.E.S.			
	Av.+ and Av.		*Av.— and D*	
	Interested	*Uninterested*	*Interested*	*Uninterested*
	%	%	%	%
1950 Vote				
Conservative	63	59	26	22
Labour	22	20	65	64
Liberal	10	14	4	3
Did not vote	5	7	5	11
N. (=100%)	(106)	(44)	(271)	(324)

Attention in this chapter has been concentrated on change of opinion. We have taken the vote intentions expressed in December as a starting point, and asked which groups were most likely to change their minds before polling day, or to fail to vote. We have seen that change was more frequent among the politically uninterested, among women and older people, and among those whose original vote intention differed from that of the majority of members of their social class (measured by a number of different indices), or organisations to which they belonged (trade unions), and of their primary groups (family, friends and co-workers).

But this focus on change may lead to neglect of what is probably the most important fact about political allegiances —that the large majority of people do not change. 77% of the sample voted on polling day for the party they had named ten weeks before. This proportion of constants varied between the different groups which have been examined. In some it was very much higher, but even among those most likely to change, the proportion of constants never fell below 70%. (The lowest figures were for the politically uninterested, and for those whose families were divided in their choice of party.)

If the emphasis has so far been placed on change rather

than on constancy, changes have also been traced only in one of the two possible directions. Instead of taking vote intentions as a starting point, we might have taken the final vote and asked how many of the people who voted for each party had decided on their vote ten weeks before the election. The vote for each of the major parties was in fact made up of a large majority whose decision had been taken long before polling day (our data only go back ten weeks, but it is certain that for many people the decision had been taken years before), and a minority who decided during the campaign period. 88% of those who voted Conservative, and 84% of those who voted Labour had already made up their minds how they would vote before our field work was started. As a way of summarising earlier findings and putting the discussion of change into better perspective, and because of its intrinsic interest, Table 55 compares the composition of the reliable majority whose decision had been made early, and of the hesitant minority who made up their minds late, for each of the major parties.

In class composition, by whatever index is used, constant Conservatives included a higher proportion of middle class people than hesitant Conservatives, and constant Labour voters a higher proportion of working-class people than hesitant Labour voters. For both parties, the constants were more likely than the changers to be men, although the difference is greater for Labour voters. Constant Labour voters included a much higher proportion in the youngest age group, people under 30, than did Labour changers; while constant Conservatives were more likely to be middle aged (30 to 49). For both parties there were higher proportions of people over 50 among the changers than among the constants. Among Conservative voters, constants were less likely than changers to be union members, while among Labour voters the reverse is true—constants were considerably more likely than changers to be union members. Finally, constant voters for both parties were more interested in politics than were hesitant voters.

Table 55*

SOCIAL CHARACTERISTICS OF CONSTANT AND CHANGING VOTERS

1950 Vote Vote compared to V.I.	Conservative		Labour	
	Constant %	Changed %	Constant %	Changed %
S.E.S.				
Av.+ and Av.	43	11	6	19
Av.−	51	85	81	65
D	6	4	13	16
Hall-Jones grade				
1–4	36	15	3	16
5–7	47	52	88	77
Unclassifiable	17	33	9	7
Self-assigned class				
Upper middle & middle	47	15	4	18
Lower middle	16	22	5	7
Working	33	56	87	68
Don't know	4	7	4	7
Sex				
Men	40	38	53	37
Women	60	62	47	63
Age				
21–29	18	19	29	12
30–49	37	27	45	51
50–65	25	31	18	24
65 and over	20	23	8	13
School-leaving age				
14 and under	54	73	86	82
15 and over	46	27	14	18
Trade union membership				
Member	21	28	47	25
Non-member	43	36	24	34
Not-working	36	36	29	41
Interested in politics				
Interested	60	45	52	26
Uninterested	40	55	48	74
N. (=100%)	(203)	(27)	(348)	(68)

Who Were the Changers?

* In studying Table 55, it must be borne in mind that the 'changers' are not homogeneous groups, and that the frequency of different types of change is not the same for both parties. Conservative changers include people whose first vote intention was Labour and who were undecided in equal numbers, and a smaller group who changed from the Liberal Party. Labour changers include more than twice as many of the originally undecided as of converts from the Conservative Party and, again, a smaller group of temporary Liberals. It is not possible, because of the smallness of the sample, to separate these groups, but the party differences account for some of the contrasts between Conservative and Labour changers, notably the high proportion of women among Labour changers. Many of them had voted Labour in 1945, and possibly never had any serious thoughts of changing parties. The numbers of changers of each type for the two parties were: Conservative: 11 from Labour, 5 from Liberal, 11 from don't know; Labour: 18 from Conservative, 6 from Liberal, 44 from don't know.

Chapter Thirteen

POLITICAL ISSUES AND PARTY
LOYALTY

I N the previous chapter, the findings of the Greenwich
survey on the question '*Who* were most likely to change
their minds during the election campaign about how
they were going to vote?' were outlined. In the present
chapter, some tentative answers will be suggested to the much
more difficult and complex question 'Why?' The associations
between views on political issues and change of opinion will
be examined.

At the same time, a change in the focus of attention will
be made. In discussing the change tables given previously,
attention was concentrated on the groups which were most
likely to abandon their original vote intention, rather than
on those most likely to remain constant. This was to some
extent an arbitrary choice, and it has been pointed out that
both sides of the relationship must be borne in mind when
looking for interpretative hypotheses. But in discussing the
relationship between views on particular political issues and
change of vote intention, attention will be focused mainly on
the groups most likely to remain constant. The reason for
this is simply that it is on this side of the relationship that our
data most easily 'make sense'. The tables presented below
suggest positive reasons why people remain loyal to their
party, but for the most part only negative reasons why they
change.

This difference is probably in part due to the choice of
questions put to informants during the interview. In part,

Political Issues and Party Loyalty

also, it may be due to the fact that we were studying change during an election campaign, when, as we have seen, the changers were likely to be people with little interest in politics. Such people were perhaps less clearly aware of the reasons for their choice of party, or less able to explain them, than were the interested. Finally, and most important, our sample was too small and the changers too few to enable us to distinguish between change of different types and in different directions. But, for example, people who moved from the Conservative Party to the Liberal Party probably had different reasons for changing from those held by people who switched to the Labour Party. The eventual non-voters were different again. We cannot study these small groups of changers statistically, but we can compare those who remained loyal to their party with those who did not.

We shall first look at the relationship between opinions and change on a very general level, using the Index of Political Opinion, which summarises our informants' views on ten statements taken from the election manifestos of the two major parties. In Table 56 we have singled out informants who told us that they intended to vote for the Conservatives or for the Labour Party and divided them into groups whose opinions accorded in varying degrees with the official standpoint of their party. We have then compared their final vote with their earlier vote intention.

Table 56

POLITICAL OPINION SCORE AND CHANGE OF VOTE INTENTION

	Vote Intention						
	Conservative				Labour		
Opinion Score	Strong Cons.	Mod. Cons.	Neutral	Cons.	Neutral	Mod. Lab.	Strong Lab.
Vote compared to V.I.	(10 – 7)	(6 – 3)	(2 – —2)	(10 – 3)	(2 – —2)	(—3 – —6)	(—7 – —10)
	%	%	%	%	%	%	%
Same party	93	84	67	73	86	92	96
Other party	2	13	21	23	6	2	4
Did not vote	5	3	12	4	8	6	—
N. (= 100%)	(60)	(101)	(88)	(22)	(22)	(137)	(28)

There is nothing surprising in the fact shown here that the stronger a person's agreement with the propositions of his own party the less likely he is to change his mind and vote for another party. What is perhaps surprising is that almost three-quarters of those who, in general, disagreed with their party on the statements summarised in the index, nevertheless voted for it. Loyalty to a party appears to be compatible with almost any degree of disagreement with its formal election policies.[1] (One person who intended to vote Conservative, for example, held opinions which placed him in the Strongly Labour group, with a score of -7. He nevertheless voted Conservative.)

Undoubtedly the issues summarised in this Political Opinion Index were not all equally important. However, the tabulation of change against opinions on the ten individual items gives a confusing picture, from which no clear conclusions emerge. The complete cross-tabulation is in Appendix C, where reasons for the fact that it does not throw much light on the relationship between opinions and party loyalty are suggested. (Other negative findings are also given in Appendix C.)

Of all the questions on political opinions and attitudes to the parties asked in the course of the survey, the one whose replies show the strongest association with constancy of vote intention is the question on which political problems informants thought were the most important. We have seen that voters for the two major parties agreed that housing and the cost of living were among the most important problems, but that Conservative voters stressed nationalisation and taxation as next in importance, while for Labour voters unemployment was even more important than housing, and the Health Service considerably more important than either nationalisation or taxation.

In giving these replies, informants said which problems they considered most important, but they were not asked what they thought should be done about them. The policy implications of selecting some of them as important are ambiguous if the political views of the person making the

[1] These were, however, omissions from our lists. See Appendix C.

selection are not taken into account. A Conservative who
thought nationalisation important probably meant at least
that no further industries should be nationalised and perhaps that those already nationalised should be returned to
private ownership. A Labour voter who thought nationalisation important may have meant that further industries
should be taken over by the State as soon as possible. There
are similar possibilities of ambiguity in other cases. But the
translation of replies into very broad policy recommendations
can probably safely be made for the four groups with whom
we shall be particularly concerned: Conservatives who
thought nationalisation and taxation important, and Labour
voters who thought unemployment and the Health Service
important. In the following discussion, Conservatives who
stressed the first two problems will be interpreted to mean
'There should be no more nationalisation', and 'Taxation
should be reduced'; and Labour voters who stressed the
second two problems will be taken to mean 'Unemployment
should be prevented', and 'The Health Service should be
maintained'. For the replies of some individuals, these trans-
lations are doubtless too mild, but they can scarcely be said
to be too extreme.

Replies to the question can thus be taken to indicate
differences between voters for the two parties in the relative
value placed on various political aims. These differences
distinguish social classes as well as supporters of the two
political parties. It was chiefly the middle-class Conservatives who stressed the importance of nationalisation and
taxation. The number of middle-class Labour voters in the
second-interview sample is too small for a similar comparison
to be made between middle-class and working-class Labour
voters, but the latter certainly placed more importance on
unemployment and the Health Service than did either group
of Conservative voters. The percentages of each class-vote
group who named the problems under discussion among the
three they considered most important are shown in Table 57.

Views on which political problems were most important
can, then, be taken as indicating differences in the relative
values placed on certain broad political ends between voters

for each of the major parties, differences which appear to characterise particularly the middle-class majority of Conservative voters and the working-class majority of Labour voters. Table 58 shows the relationship between these differences in value and stability of vote intention. Informants have been divided into those who included a particular problem among the three they considered most important and those who did not, and by vote intention, and the amount of change in each of the resulting groups compared. This has been done successively for each of the four problems on which voters for the two parties differed in their estimates of value.

Table 57

VOTE INTENTION, CLASS AND VIEWS ON THE IMPORTANCE OF CERTAIN ELECTION PROBLEMS

	Vote Intention			
	Conservative		*Labour*	
Self-assigned class	*Middle*	*Working*	*Middle**	*Working*
	%	%	%	%
Problems named				
Cost of living	52	66	66	58
Housing	52	56	66	50
Nationalisation	45	18	33	18
Taxation	38	22	7	8
Unemployment	25	38	40	59
Health Service	8	10	47	33
N. (=100%)	(71)	(50)	(15)	(109)

* These figures are included only for the sake of symmetry. The number is too small to give any indication of the difference from other groups.

Among those who started out intending to vote Conservative, people who placed importance on the two problems stressed more by Conservatives than by Labour voters—nationalisation and taxation—were the more likely to remain faithful to their party. Among Labour intenders, opinions about the importance of these two issues made little difference. Among those who started out intending to vote Labour, people who placed importance on unemployment and the Health Service were the more likely to remain faithful to their

Political Issues and Party Loyalty

Table 58

CHANGE AND VIEWS ON THE IMPORTANCE OF CERTAIN ELECTION PROBLEMS

	Conservative		Labour	
	Yes	*No*	*Yes*	*No*
(a) *Nationalisation Important?**	%	%	%	%
1950 Vote				
Same as V.I.†	93	74	96	92
Other party	5	20	4	5
Did not vote	2	6	—	3
N. (=100%)	(44)	(82)	(28)	(102)
(b) *Taxation Important?**				
1950 Vote				
Same as V.I.	96	74	90	92
Other party	2	20	—	5
Did not vote	2	6	10	3
N. (=100%)	(41)	(85)	(10)	(120)
(c) *Unemployment Important?**				
1950 Vote				
Same as V.I.	77	82	96	88
Other party	20	12	3	7
Did not vote	3	6	1	5
N. (=100%)	(36)	(90)	(71)	(59)
(d) *Health Service Important?**				
1950 Vote				
Same as V.I.	59	84	98	89
Other party	29	12	—	7
Did not vote	12	4	2	4
N. (=100%)	(17)	(109)	(45)	(85)

(Vote Intention header spans Conservative and Labour.)

* 'Yes' indicates that informants included this problem as one of the three most important, 'No' that they omitted it.

† The appearance of greater constancy among Labour intenders than among Conservative intenders is in part due to the method of selecting the second interview sample, on whose replies this table is based. In all, 81% of Conservative intenders and 92% of Labour intenders among this sub-sample remained constant to their vote intention. The figures for the panel as a whole are 83% for Conservative and 88% for Labour intenders.

party. On the other hand, Conservative intenders who thought these problems important were the more likely to change.[1] In short, and translated into the language suggested above, voters who stressed ends which were more highly valued by supporters of their own party than by those of the other party were more likely to remain constant to their party.

The step from the fact of a statistical association to the hypothesis of a causal connection is a notoriously dangerous one to make, but it does appear that the figures in Table 58 provide data to support a (not uncommon) theory as to why people vote as they do, and why they vote along class lines. Belief in the importance of stopping nationalisation and of reducing taxation appears to strengthen loyalty to the Conservative Party; the majority of those to whom this conclusion applies were members of the middle class. Belief in the importance of preventing unemployment and of maintaining the Health Service appears to strengthen loyalty to the Labour Party; and the majority of those to whom this conclusion applies were members of the working class.[2]

[1] Part of the evidence for the statement on p. 190 above (that one reason why our tables provide positive evidence only for why people remain faithful to their party and not for why they change, lies in the type of question asked) will now be clear. We know that the people who named each of these problems thought that they were among the three most important. We do not know how important those who did not name them thought they were. They may have considered them completely unimportant, or they may have thought them next in importance to the three issues they did name. No positive conclusion can be drawn from such vague evidence.

[2] To demonstrate the connection between class, values and political loyalty more clearly, it would have been desirable to hold social class constant in Table 58. The additional control would have reduced the number of cases in each group even more drastically. But although the groups then become very small, the relationship between values and political loyalty remains when the two groups of conformist voters are isolated. The results for working-class Conservatives appear to suggest that the relationship also holds independently of class position. The percentages who remained constant among the relevant groups are as follows (figures in brackets give the number of cases). Middle-class Conservatives who thought nationalisation important 94% (32), not important 82% (39), taxation important 93% (27), not important 84% (44); working-class Conservatives who thought nationalisation important 89% (9), not important 68% (40), taxation important 100% (8), not important 63% (38); working class Labour voters who thought unemployment important 97% (64), not important 89% (44); Health Service important 100% (36), not important 90% (72).

These four broad policy aims were not merely valued differently by the two social classes and by those intending to vote for each of the two major parties, but they have also fairly clear connections, either symbolically or in fact (or both), with class interests.

The Labour Party's nationalisation programme represented an immediate and real threat to the interests of a small number of middle-class people, a distant threat (if carried considerably further) to the interests of a larger number, and probably a symbolic threat, seen as an attack on property and independence, to the majority. The middle class also stood to gain more from a reduction in taxation than did the working class. The direction of class interests in the problem of unemployment is obvious, though here again real and symbolic interests were probably intermingled. If some working-class voters retained memories of the miseries of unemployment in the past, and others saw it as a danger in the very near future, still others may have thought it important out of sympathy for the past sufferings and possible future difficulties of fellow members of their class; for the majority unemployment may also have stood symbolically for the more general interests of the working class. Finally, the working class were probably more ready to admit the great value of the Health Service (and to attribute this to Labour Party initiative) than were the middle class.

The four issues then had all a close connection with class interests. It seems probable also that each was regarded by the group of voters who stressed it as a problem which their party leaders thought of as particularly important, on which their stand was quite clear and which (even more indubitably than other problems) they alone could be trusted to handle in the right way. There is no doubt that the Conservatives' stand on nationalisation and their strong feelings about it were well known. If we had asked suitable questions, we would doubtless have found that the Conservative Party had 'captured' the issue of opposition to nationalisation as the Labour Party had 'captured' that of preventing unemployment.[1] That the Conservative Party was similarly

[1] See above, pp. 149–51.

197

identified by public opinion with the cause of reducing taxation is highly probable. Apart from the parties' past records, the Conservatives had made the reduction of taxation one of their election battle cries, while Labour had seldom mentioned the subject. We have positive evidence that the Labour Party was credited with the greatest concern for the problem of unemployment, not only by its supporters, but also by many Conservative voters. Promises to maintain and improve the Health Service were given freely by both parties during the election campaign, but it seems unlikely that those of the Conservatives could shake the faith of Labour voters that their own party was the more seriously concerned about what was one of the principal achievements of the Labour Government.

In view of all this, the figures in Table 58 appear to suggest that among the aims which keep a voter faithful to his party (and doubtless help to draw him to it in the first place) are those:

(a) Which he feels to be important. The four issues discussed are also closely connected with his class interests, materially and symbolically.

(b) Which he feels his own party is alone capable of achieving. Some of the more politically illiterate voters may have had little idea about how they were to be achieved. 16% of Labour voters did not know whether or not they agreed with the very general statement that 'Government planning is essential for full employment'.

(c) On which past party records or present party declarations are distinctive, and not easily confused with those of the rival party. This may be expressed by saying that they must form part of the party 'reputation', a reputation granted not only by its supporters but to some extent by its opponents. (Because of the strong tendency, of which we have given ample evidence, to grant all virtues to one's own party and very few to the rival party, it may be only to a slight extent.) Without this third condition, the belief in the party's ability to achieve the aim is unstable, and easily transferred to another party if the voter changes his allegiance.

The significance of this third point is brought out by the fact that there is little sign of a relationship between beliefs in the importance of the two remaining issues, the cost of living and housing, and change. The figures are shown, in a similar way as for the other four issues, in Table 59.

Table 59

CHANGE AND VIEWS ON THE IMPORTANCE
OF TWO FURTHER ELECTION PROBLEMS

	Vote Intention			
	Conservative		*Labour*	
Cost of Living Important	*Yes*	*No*	*Yes*	*No*
	%	%	%	%
1950 Vote				
Same as V.I.	78	85	91	94
Other party	18	9	5	4
Did not vote	4	6	4	2
N. (=100%)	(74)	(52)	(77)	(53)
Housing Important *1950 Vote*				
Same as V.I.	80	83	90	95
Other party	16	12	7	2
Did not vote	4	5	3	3
N. (=100%)	(69)	(57)	(67)	(63)

The cost of living and housing, although felt to be of major importance, were stressed equally by voters for both parties, and neither party had established a reputation as being the best able to handle them. People named whichever party they intended to vote for as being the most capable of handling them.[1] And, in these two cases, those who thought the problem important were not more likely than others to

[1] See Table 36 above. That answers to questions on party capabilities are most probably determined by the preference of the moment unless one party has succeeded to some extent in 'capturing' the issue is brought out by comparing the replies of constants and converts to these questions. Of the 7 people who intended to vote Labour at the time the question was asked and who later changed to another party, all 7 thought the Labour Party best fitted to handle each of the 3 problems of cost of living, housing and unemployment. Of the 9 people who intended to vote Conservative at the time the question was asked, and later changed to another party, more than half named the Conservative Party as best able to handle each problem except unemployment.

remain constant to the party for which they at first intended to vote.[1]

We have suggested that, for some voters, at least, the train of thought which connects desired ends with political parties as means to those ends can only be expressed in a very general form, for example, 'It is important to prevent unemployment, and the Labour Party will do most to prevent it.' It might be thought, in view of the actual class alignments of voting choices, that the most widely held and effective argument of this kind would run, if put into words, something like this: 'It is important to look after the interests of my class, and my party will look after them best.' We do have information about how widely held at least the second part of this argument was, in the answers, discussed in Chapter Six, to the questions about which party would do the best job for each class; although in this case we have no measure of the importance people placed on the idea of 'class interests' in general, or, rather, of the emotional force that the idea possessed for them. It has already been pointed out[2] that replies to these 'party for class' questions were similar to replies to the question on the best party to handle unemployment in that there is a tendency to allow that the Conservative Party will do the best job for the middle class and the Labour Party for the working class even among opponents of these parties.

Is it possible, then, to demonstrate the importance of the belief that 'my party will do the best job for my class' in holding voters to their party in the way we have done for other beliefs? The answer, in the case of working-class Labour voters, is 'no', since there were few of them who did not believe it. But some more indirect indications of the importance of the belief that the Labour Party serves the interests of the working class have already been given, the chief being the fact that 42% of those who intended to vote Labour made some reference to class interests in reply to a

---

[1] If anything, the reverse is true, but the differences are even smaller than those in Table 57. Of the 5 Labour intenders who thought housing important and changed parties, 4 voted Liberal and only 1 Conservative.

[2] On p. 151 above.

direct question on their reason for voting Labour. It is also worth noting that the proportion of Labour voters who said that the Labour Party would do the best job for the working class was higher (93%) even than the proportion who said it would handle unemployment best (85%).

Some Conservative voters, as we have seen, rejected the whole question of class interests, and only 75% of middle-class Conservatives stated that their party would do the best job for their own class. But they included a higher proportion who remained constant (90%) than did the few who named another party and the larger number who said they didn't know (82%).

The conclusions of this discussion may appear as obvious as the evidence presented is slight and the argument which supports it at times tenuous. Social researchers must often envy the freedom of the political commentator to speculate on the reasons for the rise and fall of parties unfettered by the need to support each point with statistics. It has nevertheless appeared worthwhile to present them. Research has often shown that generalisations which seemed obvious were false (and different things seem obvious to different people). But even where obvious generalisations are true, it is necessary to establish them in a broad sense and to redefine them in terms of research procedures before their more unexpected details (limiting conditions, variations in strength, the processes by which they come about, etc.) can be studied.

As to the imperfections of the evidence, there is little social research to which some or all of these do not apply, and they inevitably apply with much more force to study of the complex problems of the reasons for social behaviour than to the comparatively simple descriptive problems. But this does not make such research pointless. Even statistically small differences can lead to firm conclusions if they appear and reappear repeatedly in studies made at different times and places.[1] And since the findings of this and other such surveys

[1] This fact was apparently overlooked by the authors of one of the recent surveys of voting behaviour made in Great Britain, when they note that few statistically significant differences are likely to be revealed by surveys of a size financially possible to academic research bodies, and pessimistically conclude that it is not worthwhile attempting to make such surveys.

are affected by conditions peculiar to their own time and place, such repetition is essential to the building up of a body of knowledge of more general validity. Perhaps even more important, positive findings, however tentative or slight, can help future research workers to find the most useful ways of approach and avoid sterile paths. Social research is a co-operative endeavour in which progress can only be made by taking into account the successes and the failures of what has already been attempted.

Appendix A

THE COMPOSITION OF THE SECOND INTERVIEW SAMPLE

FROM the 856 persons interviewed in December 1949, 450 were selected for the second interview during the fortnight preceding polling day. The 450 included all those whose vote intention differed from their 1945 vote, those who were undecided about how they would vote, and those who had been too young to vote in 1945; and random selections of consistent Conservative and Labour supporters, and of the 1945 non-voters.

Of these 450, 10 had moved or died since our first interview, and of the remainder we managed to catch only 363 at their homes. The effective sample was again diminished when, at the post-election interview, we failed to reach 26 of those who had been given the first two interviews. Since we are primarily interested in the experiences which lead up to the final vote decision, our analysis of the second interview has been based on the 337 cases whom we interviewed on all three occasions. In the table below, their political composition is compared with that of the total sample (omitting, here also, those whom we did not reach with the post-election interview). The classification is based on a comparison of 1945 vote and December vote intention.

Three groups were over-represented in the second interview sample: those who had changed parties since 1945, those who had not made up their minds in December how they would vote, and the first voters. The emphasis on these three groups was made largely at the expense of the consistent

Labour supporters, the only group to be seriously under-represented. Consistent Conservative supporters and 1945 non-voters appeared in approximately their true proportions.

CHANGES BETWEEN 1945 VOTE AND FIRST VOTE INTENTION

	Sub-sample		Total Sample	
	No.	%	*No.*	%
Consistent Conservative	64	19	155	20
Consistent Labour	65	19	274	36
Consistent Liberal	—	—	1	*
Vote intention different to 1945 vote	46	14	53	7
Too young to vote in 1945	47	14	53	7
Undecided in December	55	16	78	10
Did not vote in 1945	60	18	154	20
Total	337	100	768†	100

(Note: The last three categories overlap. Cases which might have been classified in one of two ways have always been placed in the first appropriate group on the list.)   *=less than 1%

† 13 cases for which information was incomplete have been omitted.

Since the above table does not show the complete distribution of answers to our question on vote intention, this is given below, together with a comparison of the final 1950 vote for the sub-sample and the total sample.

FIRST VOTE INTENTION AND 1950 VOTE

	Sub-Sample	Total Sample
	%	%
1st Vote Intention		
Conservative	38	32
Labour	39	51
Liberal	6	4
Don't know	17	10
No reply	*	3
1950 Vote		
Conservative	34	30
Labour	51	54
Liberal	6	5
Did not vote	7	8
No reply	2	3
*=less than 1%	(337)	(781)

Appendix A

The table giving first vote intention shows that the second interview sample under-represented the Labour supporters and over-represented Conservative supporters and the undecided. These party differences still remained at the time of our post-poll interview, but they had been greatly reduced, partly by switches from one party to another, but more notably because 6 out of 10 of the 'don't knows' included in the second interview sample finally voted Labour. Non-voters were no more numerous in the second interview sample than in the total sample.

The distribution of other basic characteristics for the two groups is shown below:

CHARACTERISTICS OF SUB-SAMPLE AND
TOTAL SAMPLE

	Sub-Sample %	Total Sample %
Sex		
Men	44	46
Women	56	54
Age		
21–29	26	22
30–49	42	42
50–64	18	22
65 and over	14	14
Socio-economic status		
Av.+ and Av.	21	21
Av.–	69	67
D	10	12
Interest in Politics		
Very interested	11	11
Moderately interested	40	39
Not very interested	43	45
Don't know	6	5
N. (=100%)	(337)	(781)

There was a higher proportion of women among those interviewed during the campaign (since women were more likely to change their minds, and more likely to be undecided about their vote intention), and a higher proportion of the youngest age group (since we attempted to interview all first voters). These differences are, however, small in comparison with the differences in party choice. Differences in socio-economic status and in interest in politics were also small.

Since we have in almost all cases where we have presented data from the second interview held political allegiance constant, the differences between the two samples appear to be unlikely to bias our findings to any great extent.

Appendix B

THE SURVEY FIGURES ON FINAL VOTE COMPARED WITH OFFICIAL RESULTS

D URING the two weeks which followed polling day the members of our panel were interviewed for the last time. On this occasion, we reached 839 persons out of the 1,022 drawn in the original sample, and of these 781 had been interviewed previously, and 58 were reached for the first time. The questionnaire was short, and the most important items were questions on whether our informants had voted and for whom.

How does the report on their vote given by our sample compare with the official election returns for Greenwich? The figures are shown in the table below.

A COMPARISON OF VOTING BY THE PANEL AND THE TOTAL CONSTITUENCY

	Panel %	Constituency %
Reeves (Labour)	54	48
Gilbey (Conservative)	30	30
Dale (Liberal)	5	5
Did not vote	8	17
Information refused	3	—
N. (=100%)	(839)	(61,198)

Compared with the official returns for the constituency, the replies of our panel to the question about how they had voted show an unduly high proportion of Labour voters, and an unduly low proportion of non-voters. These differences are too great to be attributed solely to sampling error. What, then, has caused the discrepancies? There are three major possibilities.

Firstly, while the figures in our table representing votes received by each of the three parties are based on the count of votes cast on election day, that representing non-voters is based on the electoral roll, and is therefore not completely up to date. In our sample, itself drawn from the electoral roll, 81 persons, or 8% of the total sample, were reported by our interviewers as dead or moved from their recorded address. If this number is added to the proportion who admitted that they did not vote, we arrive at a proportion of non-voters almost the same for the panel as for the constituency. 8% is perhaps too high an estimate of the proportion of the total constituency who had moved or died. (In our sample, the 8% doubtless includes some who had merely moved to a different address in Greenwich.) But it is safe to say that a large part of the difference in the figures for non-voting is due to the fact that non-voters in our sample were all living in Greenwich at the time of the election, whereas some of those included in the figures for the whole constituency had died or moved elsewhere. When the distribution of votes alone is compared, our sample approximates more closely to the official returns :

THE DISTRIBUTION OF VOTES IN THE PANEL AND THE CONSTITUENCY

	Panel	*Constituency*
	%	%
Reeves (Labour)	61	58
Gilbey (Conservative)	34	36
Dale (Liberal)	5	6
N. (=100%)	(747)	(50,782)

A second reason for the difference may be found in the

'mortality' from the sample. After excluding those who had in fact died, or who had moved, we obtained post-election interviews with 89% of our sample. Possibly the 11% whom we were unable to interview differed in some important respect from those who were interviewed. This hypothesis can be partially tested, since three-quarters of those whom we missed in the post-election poll were interviewed at least once before the election.

Compared with those who were interviewed after the election, the 75 people whom we missed on this occasion, but about whom we have some information, were slightly more likely to be women (57% as compared to 53%), and to belong to the D socio-economic grade (14% as compared to 11%). There was little difference in age. In December, higher proportions of them had intended to vote Conservative or had not known how they would vote, and a lower proportion had intended to vote Labour than among the remainder of the sample. The proportions are shown in the following table.

VOTE INTENTIONS OF THOSE INCLUDED
AND NOT INCLUDED IN POST ELECTION
POLL

First Vote Intention	Interviewed after election %	Not Interviewed after election %
Conservative	32	36
Labour	51	42
Liberal	4	4
Don't know	10	15
No reply	3	3
N. (=100%)	(781)	(75)

It seems likely, therefore, that those whom we did not interview after the election included higher proportions both of Conservatives and non-voters. (Women were both more Conservative and more likely not to vote than men; and those who had no settled vote intention in December included a particularly high proportion who eventually did

14   209

not vote.) Mortality from the original sample thus accounts for part at least of the bias in results.

A third factor which may have been a contributory cause is the possibility that some informants did not tell the truth. We have no means of checking on this. In the Elmira survey, made in the United States during the 1948 election, it was found that 'about 9% of the individuals who told the interviewers that they had voted, had in fact not done so. This was established by referring to the Election Board records. Some had not registered and therefore could not vote; others, though registered, did not cast their ballots on Election Day.'[1] It may well be the case in our survey also that some informants told us they had voted when in fact they had not done so. The wide recognition of a duty to vote is illustrated by the reasons given for not voting by those who admitted that they had failed to do so. Two-thirds of them claimed that they were prevented by external causes (by far the most common was illness), and only one-third gave subjective reasons such as 'too tired', 'too busy', 'couldn't be bothered', 'didn't think my party would get in anyway'. It seems quite likely that some of our informants would be ashamed to admit that they had not voted. However, unlike the Elmira survey, our questionnaire approached the question of whether the informant had voted in a roundabout way, to make it more difficult to give an untruthful answer. It is also possible that some people told our interviewers that they had voted for one party when in fact they had voted for another, perhaps wanting to appear to have voted for the winning side. These possibilities cannot be checked, but it seems unlikely that they operated to any large extent, since the bias in our sample is adequately explained by other factors.

Finally there is the 3% who would not tell us whether or for what party they had voted. Most of this small group of 23 people probably either voted Conservative or did not vote. In December their vote intentions had been Conservative 6, Labour 2, Liberal 2, don't know 10, no reply 3.

To summarise this discussion the difference in voting be-

[1] Alice S. Kitt and David B. Gleicher, 'Determinants of Voting Behavior', *Public Opinion Quarterly*, Vol. 14, No. 3, Fall 1950, p. 407.

tween our sample and the constituency as a whole appears to
be primarily due, on the one hand, to the fact that the electoral roll included people who have been classed as non-
voters but who were no longer living in the constituency;
and on the other to the fact that those who were not interviewed or who refused to reply to our questions included
high proportions of groups who voted Conservative, and
who did not vote at all.

Appendix C

ADDITIONAL DATA ON OPINIONS AND CHANGE OF VOTE INTENTION

REFERENCES were made in Chapter 13 to the association between change of vote intention and opinions on some of the ten statements which were selected from the party election programmes. (For a list of the statements and an account of how they were selected see pp. 139–40.) The table on p. 213 shows the association for all ten statements. The figures give the percentages who remained constant to their December vote intention among those who agreed, disagreed or had no opinion on each of these statements.

Apart from the fact that those who agreed with their party were more likely to vote for it than those who disagreed, a finding neither new nor particularly informative, no clear pattern emerges from the figures. Few issues stand out as particularly strongly associated either with change or with loyalty, and in the case of those which do stand out, the most probable explanation is one which throws little light on the problem of the relationship between issues and change. Conservative intenders who agreed with the Labour Party over nationalisation and full employment were particularly inconstant. But these issues cannot be taken as a reason for change to Labour, since only a fraction of the informants concerned voted Labour. And Conservative intenders who disagreed with their own party over building controls were also less constant. Since it is unlikely that the Conservative

PARTY CONSTANCY AND OPINIONS ON POLICY STATEMENTS

Figures show percentages in each group whose final vote was the same as their vote intention. Bases for percentages are given in brackets.

1st Vote Intention

Opinions on statements	Conservative			Labour		
	Agree	*Disagree*	*Don't know*	*Agree*	*Disagree*	*Don't know*
Conservative Statements						
Building controls	86 (198)	67 (24)	74 (19)	86 (170)	93 (144)	82 (69)
State trading	84 (193)	82 (11)	74 (38)	85 (115)	93 (145)	86 (126)
Closed shop	85 (171)	79 (24).	78 (46)	87 (166)	92 (127)	85 (93)
Socialism	85 (167)	80 (36)	77 (39)	86 (81)	90 (219)	86 (86)
Empire first	83 (92)	65 (17)	88 (33)	88 (250)	96 (46)	83 (91)
Labour Statements						
Full employment	75 (109)	91 (92)	83 (41)	89 (305)	88 (17)	84 (63)
Workers' control	78 (73)	87 (124)	79 (43)	91 (241)	92 (75)	77 (68)
Equality	79 (85)	88 (113)	79 (42)	90 (236)	87 (77)	92 (77)
Nationalisation	47 (17)	87 (209)	73 (15)	95 (192)	84 (117)	78 (76)
Native self-government	78 (90)	92 (82)	80 (69)	90 (209)	92 (63)	84 (114)

attack on building controls 'boomeranged' and convinced people that Labour would build more houses than the Conservatives, this difference can be more easily taken as an index of already feeble Conservative support than as a reason for change. Among Labour intenders, the most likely to change were in most cases those who had no opinion at all. The issues most strongly associated with constancy to the original party have been discussed in Chapter Thirteen. To these should be added that Labour intenders who agreed with the statement that 'All basic industries should be nationalised' included a high proportion of constants. This finding was also suggested by the figures in the table on p. 213. Approval of nationalisation on the part of Labour intenders could probably be added to the list of aims which strengthen party loyalty discussed in Chapter Thirteen.

The table does, however, suggest reasons why the question on 'important problems' revealed stronger differences in party loyalty than did this series of items. Firstly, the statements were difficult for some informants to understand. This accounts for the fact that the least constant among Labour intenders were those with no opinion, i.e. the politically uninterested. Secondly, there was no measure of how strongly informants felt on the particular issues. This accounts for the fact that the statement on nationalisation did not distinguish loyal Conservatives, nor the statement on full employment the loyal Labour voters. Nearly all Conservatives rejected the former statement, including presumably many who did not feel very strongly about it; and nearly all Labour voters accepted the latter statement, also presumably including many who did not feel strongly.

The third reason goes deeper than these. The two most conspicuous omissions from the list, if they are to be regarded as summaries of party propaganda during the election campaign, are statements on taxation and on the social services. The reason for these omissions is provided by the criteria of selection—that the statements should be unambiguously identifiable, at least by people with considerable political knowledge, as coming from one party or the other. At least on the Health Service, it would have been difficult to find a statement of which this would be true. Nevertheless, as we have suggested in Chapter Thirteen, the cause of reducing taxation may have been popularly identified with the Conservative Party, and that of maintaining the Health Service with the Labour Party. Such popular identifications could well exist even when, at that particular time, official party pronouncements were indistinguishable from each other. Indeed, the more successful a policy has been, the more likely it is that this situation will occur.

If this is so, then lists of statements selected on the principles we used will be of little use in research designed to discover the most influential issues. The Greenwich survey findings suggest that the most useful approach is likely to be not that of asking people what they think about what the parties say, but of asking what they themselves think on the issues of political debate. This must be done without giving direct cues as to what the 'party line' answer is. Our questions on 'which party can do this or that best?' were of limited usefulness, because the only alternatives were a 'loyal' answer, a 'disloyal' answer, or no answer at all.

One further negative finding will be mentioned, concerning expectations of victory and change of vote intention. The assumption behind the relentless optimism of most election propaganda, however intellectual or objective its tone, is that people are more likely to vote for a party if they think it is going to win. We asked informants which party they thought would win the election in Greenwich, and throughout the country. Those who thought their own party would win were no more likely to remain constant to their vote intention than were those who thought the opposition would win.

Appendix D

THE FLOATING VOTE

IN Chapters Twelve and Thirteen the findings of the Greenwich Survey on factors associated with constancy to a party and with changes of party were reported. These findings do not go very far towards explaining the swing towards Conservatism in 1950, or towards indicating the causes of electoral swings in general. The chief conclusion of the discussion about 'who' changed was that changers were found more often among those whose original vote intention deviated from that of the majority of their social group. The personal pressures for conformity hinted at here may well vary in strength for different groups under different circumstances, so that the process may have relevance for understanding variations in party fortunes. But while this may happen, we have no data on the nature of the conditioning circumstances. Our figures suggest some of the factors associated with change as such, but not with change in any particular direction.

On the other hand, the data on opinions indicate some of the beliefs associated with party loyalty. But even if the conclusions of Chapter Thirteen are accepted, they doubtless indicate only a few of the many reasons involved, the evidence about changers is purely negative, and there is no way of weighing up the relative advantages to each party of the appeals discussed.

There are many facts which explain why little could be said about reasons for change. There were too few changes in the sample to enable us to differentiate between different types and different directions of change. Even had this been possible the sample would still have been too small to study the reasons held by different sub-groups, although there are almost certainly important variations. A final fact is that our field work was begun after the important changes had taken place.

A common conclusion about the 1950 election, which is supported by our own evidence and by that of other opinion polls,[1] is that Labour support began to decline and Conservative prestige to rise fairly soon after the 1945 General Election. These changes continued slowly until sometime towards the end of 1949, but with increasing talk of an election in the near future the process was reversed. If this is so, we would need to trace changes in attitude and in party support further back than is possible with our data, in order to explain the 1945 swing to the Conservatives. The most we can do is give a brief and very general analysis of the differences between our informants' votes in 1950, and their reports about how they voted in 1945.

In 1950 the Greenwich Labour candidate was returned with a reduced percentage of the total votes cast, compared with 1945. The Conservative candidate gained an increased percentage, in spite of the fact that there was a Liberal candidate standing in addition to the candidates of the two parties which had contested the seat in 1945. Results for the two elections are compared below.

THE DISTRIBUTION OF VOTES IN GREENWICH, 1945 AND 1950

	1945 %	*1950* %
Labour	66	58
Conservative	34	36
Liberal	—	6
Total (=100%)	(33,658)	(50,782)

[1] See, e.g., the results cited by H. G. Nicholas, *The British General Election of 1950*, p. 284.

Our discussion of the 'floating vote' must inevitably be less reliable than our discussion of pre-election changes in vote intention. Our record of our informants' 1945 vote is based on answers to a question asked four and a half years after the event, and is unlikely to be entirely accurate. But we can get some indication of the reliability of their answers, since the question about 1945 vote was repeated in our second interview. The following table compares the answers given on the two occasions.

A COMPARISON OF THE ANSWERS TO TWO QUESTIONS ON 1945 VOTE

	First Interview				
	Conservative	Labour	Liberal	Did not vote	Too young
Second Interview	%	%	%	%	%
Conservative	88	8	—	8	—
Labour	4	87	—	33	7
Liberal	3	—	100	—	—
Did not vote	5	5	—	56	2
Too young	—	—	—	3	91
N. (=100%)	(77)	(118)	(1)	(75)	(46)

The proportion who gave identical replies to the question on the two occasions is highest for those who said that they had voted in 1945, and for those voting for the first time; but even among these groups, between 9% and 13% gave a different reply on the second occasion. It is lowest for those who at first said that they had not voted in 1945. Only 56% of them repeated this reply on the second occasion. In all, 81% of the sample gave the same reply on both occasions.

The changes in answer were not entirely random. Among those who gave different replies on the two occasions, 60% altered their answer so that on the second occasion it was identical with their final vote. This suggests that the effect of the election campaign, in heightening political partisanship, had been to make people project their present allegiances into the past. There is, of course, no way of telling whether a similar distortion had already taken place when we asked the question for the first time in December, nor, if it had, how great the distortion was. It seems likely, however, that a process of this kind operated to some extent. If this is so, we are more likely, using the information we have, to under-estimate than to over-estimate the amount of change between the elections.

We have one more comforting probability to set against these reflections. The replies about 1945 vote are likely to be somewhat more reliable for our total sample than for the second interview sub-sample on which the table above is based. The latter included a higher proportion of those who changed their minds during the campaign, and the changers were less likely than the constants to give consistent replies about their 1945 vote. (85% of those who remained constant to one party during the campaign, and 66% of the changers gave consistent replies.)

In view of all this, any conclusion based on our information about 1945 vote must be regarded with considerable caution. It nevertheless seems worthwhile to use it as the basis for a brief analysis of the 1945–50 floating vote. (The difficulty and expense of making a panel survey covering the whole period between two elections would be enormous, and it seems unlikely that anyone will undertake such a task for a long while to come.)

We shall use 'floating vote' in a wide but negative sense to include all informants except those whose vote in 1950 was the same as in 1945—all except the constants. Most discussion of the floating vote is centred on the people who are assumed to have changed from one party to another. But the next table in which the 1945–50 changes are, as a first step, classified without reference to party, shows that in Greenwich the party-changers made up only about a quarter of all changers.

Those who had not voted in 1945 were more than twice as numerous as those who changed parties, even if we do not include among them the 6% of our sample who were too young to vote in 1945. 1945 was an election with a particularly low turnout, due at least in part to failure to reach all service voters and others displaced because of the war; the turnout in 1950 was unusually high. It is impossible therefore to draw conclusions of general significance from these figures, but they do suggest that the 'marginal' voters may play a more important role in electoral swings than is often recognised, and emphasise the need to base speculation about their causes on figures of turnover.

VOTE CHANGES, 1945–50

	% of total sample	% of 1950 voters
1950 Voters		
Voted for same party 1945–50	54	61
Changed parties 1945–50	9	10
Did not vote 1945 although eligible	19	21
Too young to vote 1945	6	7
No reply about 1945 vote	1	1
1950 Non-Voters		
Voted in 1945	4	
Did not vote 1945	3	
Too young to vote 1945	*	
No reply about 1945 vote	1	
Information on 1950 vote refused	3	
N. (=100%)	(781)	(697)

* Less than 1%.

How did these changes affect the fortunes of the parties? On p. 221 we give the details of voting turnover between the two elections.

The politically constant formed a substantial majority of the voters for each of the major parties, although, as we would expect in view of the swing towards the Conservatives, the proportion was higher for the Labour Party. The remainder of the vote for each major party was made up of gains from three sources: the 1945 non-voters, the other major party (gains from the Liberal Party were negligible), and the first voters. Against these must be balanced losses of three kinds: through non-voting in 1950, to the other major party, and to the Liberals. Because the electorate had increased in size since 1945, and because of the low turnout in 1945, the total number of votes gained by each party outweighed their losses. Labour gains, in absolute numbers, were larger than Conservative gains, but their losses were also larger, so that on balance the two parties increased their vote by an approximately equal number of electors. However, in proportion to its 1945 share of the total vote, the increase was relatively greater for the Conservative Party than for the Labour Party, and accounted for its increased percentage.[1]

1950 VOTE ANALYSED BY 1945 VOTE

	1950 Vote			
	Conservative %	*Labour* %	*Liberal* %	*Did not vote* %
1945 Vote				
Conservative	61	4	19	8
Labour	10	66	45	38
Liberal	*	*	5	—
Did not vote	21	21	26	44
Too young	5	8	5	8
No reply	3	1	—	2
N. (=100%)	(337)	(422)	(38)	(61)

* Less than 1%.

The largest gain for both parties was from the 1945 non-voters. But whereas Labour gains were almost twice as great as Conservative gains from this source, its losses through non-voting in 1950 of people who had voted in 1945 were almost eight times as great, and almost cancelled out the advantage.

The two groups of non-voters (1945 and 1950) were very

[1] Some of the factors limiting the accuracy of this analysis have already been discussed. But it should be further pointed out that our sample, while as nearly representative of the Greenwich electorate in 1950 as we could make it, is not representative of the Greenwich electorate in 1945. We have taken no account of migration into and out of the constituency, nor of deaths. Since older people more often vote Conservative, this last factor is likely to have resulted in a greater loss to the Conservatives than to the Labour Party.

different in composition. Half of those who did not vote in 1945 were men, and more than 8 out of 10 were under 50 years old. Of those who did not vote in 1950 but had voted in 1945, two-thirds were women and two-thirds aged 50 or more. Both politically and socially, the 1950 non-voters are probably much more typical of the marginal fringe of people who vote only occasionally, since wartime dislocations affected the 1945 turnout.

Switches from one party to another were by no means all in one direction, but the balance was in favour of the Conservative Party. The Labour Party lost more than twice as many votes to the Liberals as the Conservatives did, and there were three people who changed from Labour to Conservative for every two who changed from Conservative to Labour. Finally, Labour gained a higher proportion of the young voters than did the Conservatives.

These complex changes are difficult to summarise. Sources of advantage to the Conservatives, in order of importance, appear to have been: non-voting by 1945 Labour supporters, Labour loss to the Liberals, and switches between the two major parties. These were offset, in absolute numbers but not in proportion to the increased size of the electorate, by Labour gains from 1945 non-voters and from the first voters.

INDEX

223

Index

McCallum, R. B., 3n.
Maine, Sir Henry, 14
Manchester University studies, 3 and n.
Mandate, 15
Martin, F. M., 118n., 119
Meetings, 8off.
  attendance at, 27
  audience for, 155ff., 178
  open-air, 85-6
Merriam, C. E., 4 and n.
Middle class, meaning, 103n.
Ministry, election in relation to, 18
Motives, difficulties of enquiry concerning, 100

Names, use of, in speeches, 82-3
Names of candidates, knowledge of, 157-8
Nationalisation, 66, 140-2, 148, 193-7
Newspapers,
  electors and, 162-6
  and political interest, 136-7, 138, 162ff.
Nicholas, H. G., 3 and n., 9, 160n., 163, 217n.
Nominations, 92
Nonconformist vote, 111
Non-rational choice, 5, 7
Non-voters, composition of group, 221-2
Nuffield College Studies, 3 and n.

Objects of survey, 1
Officers, party, 5off.
Opinion,
  change of, see Vote intention
  common, between parties, 142
  public and group, 142
  see also Public opinion
Opinion polls, 4-5
Organisation, political, study of, 26-7

Palmer, E. T., 56
'Panel' technique, 3-4

Parties,
  main points of disagreement, 140
  membership, 45ff.
  officers, 49
  in relation to election, 18-19
Party
  and public opinion, 15
  and self-assigned class, 119
  see also Commitment; Constancy
Party allegiance, changes in, 131
Party members, degree of political interest of, 48-9
Party membership, 36, 37
Party supporters, forms of help given by, 132
Policy statements, party, 139-40
  views on, 141
Politics,
  degree of interest in, 125ff.; see also Interest
  and sociology, distinction, 11-12
Posters, 80, 98
Potter, Allen, 3n.
Power,
  flow of, 12
  'ideal types', 11
Press, see Newspapers
Pressure groups, 13
Printing, cost to parties, 44
Problems, particular, and party preferences, 149-51
Propaganda,
  audience for, 155ff.
  and change of vote intention, 177-8
Prudential Staff Union, 56
Public opinion,
  and electorate, 13-15
  meaning, 14
  see also Opinion

Questionnaire, form of, 24, 25
Questions, at meetings, 83-4

Radio, and political interest, 137, 138; see also Broadcasts

Index

For Product Safety Concerns and Information please contact our EU
representative GPSR@taylorandfrancis.com
Taylor & Francis Verlag GmbH, Kaufingerstraße 24, 80331 München, Germany

www.ingramcontent.com/pod-product-compliance
Lightning Source LLC
Chambersburg PA
CBHW070404270326
41926CB00014B/2697

*9 7 8 0 4 1 5 8 6 3 2 4 7 *